This book comprises the papers presented at

The Common Good in an Unequal World:
A Conference on the
Compendium of the Social Doctrine of the Church,

which took place on 2 March 2006 in Croke Park, Dublin, and was organised by the Irish Commission for Justice and Social Affairs.

Each paper, except those by Eoin Cassidy, Patrick Hannon and John Murray, were presented on that day. Papers have been edited slightly to take into account style and clarity, but the tenets and opinions of the speakers remain as were.

The Common Good in an Unequal World

Reflections on the *Compendium of the Social Doctrine of the Church*

Edited by
Eoin G. Cassidy

VERITAS

First published 2007 by
Veritas Publications
7/8 Lower Abbey Street
Dublin 1
Ireland
Email publications@veritas.ie
Website www.veritas.ie

ISBN 978 1 84730 056 0

10 9 8 7 6 5 4 3 2 1

A catalogue record for this book is available from the British Library.

Printed in the Republic of Ireland by Betaprint, Dublin

Veritas books are printed on paper made from the wood pulp of managed forests. For every tree felled, at least one tree is planted, thereby renewing natural resources.

CONTENTS

CONTRIBUTORS

An Taoiseach Bertie Ahern has served as the eleventh Taoiseach of Ireland since 26 June 1997. Before this he held the positions of Tánaiste, Minister for Finance, for Arts, Culture and the Gaeltacht, for Industry and for Labour. He has been leader of Fianna Fáil since 1994 and was first elected to the Dáil in 1977. He represents the constituency of Dublin Central.

David Begg is General Secretary of the Irish Congress of Trade Unions. He is a Director of the Central Bank, a member of the National Economic and Social Council (NESC) and of the Council of the Economic and Social Research Institute (ESRI). He is a Governor of the Irish Times Trust. Between 1997 and 2001 he was CEO of Concern Worldwide, an international humanitarian relief and development agency.

Professor William Binchy is Regius Professor of Law at Trinity College, Dublin. He was formerly a special legal adviser on family law reform to the Irish Department of Justice and Research Counsellor to the Law Reform Commission. He is a member of the Irish Human Rights Commission. Professor Binchy has authored and co-authored books on private international law, torts and family law. He has represented Ireland at The Hague Conference on Private International Law on the themes of marriage and inter-country adoption. He was a member of the Committee on the Offences against the State Acts, chaired by the Hon. Mr Justice Anthony Hederman.

Dr Seán Brady is Archbishop of Armagh and Primate of All Ireland. He was ordained to the priesthood in 1964. In 1980 he was appointed Vice-Rector of the Irish College, Rome and in 1987 became Rector of the College, a post he held until 1993, when he returned to Ireland to become Parish Priest of Castletara, Co. Cavan. In February 1995 he was ordained Coadjutor Archbishop of Armagh, and on the retirement of Cardinal Cahal B. Daly succeeded him as Archbishop of Armagh and Primate of All Ireland on 1 October 1996. He was installed as Archbishop of Armagh on 3 November 1996. Archbishop Brady is President of the Irish Bishops' Conference, a member of its Department of Planning and Communications and a Trustee of Trócaire.

Deirdre Carroll has been CEO of Inclusion Ireland, National Association for People with an Intellectual Disability (formally NAMHI) since 2001. Prior to this she was the Assistant CEO. Her background is in Social Policy and Administration. She has degrees from University College Dublin and the London School of Economics and has worked in the voluntary sector for nearly twenty years.

Dr Eoin G. Cassidy is a priest of the Dublin Archdiocese and is Head of the Philosophy Department at the Mater Dei Institute, Dublin City University. He is chair of the International sub-committee of the Irish Commission for Justice and Social Affairs (ICJSA). Previous works include *Prosperity with a Purpose: What Purpose?* (Veritas, 2000), *Measuring Ireland:*

Discerning Values and Beliefs (Veritas, 2002) and *The Search for Meaning and Values* (Veritas, 2004).

Dr Raymond Field is Auxiliary Bishop of Dublin. He was ordained to the priesthood in 1970 and ordained Titular Bishop of Ard Mór and Auxiliary Bishop of Dublin in September 1997. Bishop Field is a member of the Department of Social Issues and International Affairs of the Bishops' Conference, Chairman of the ICJSA, and Chairman of the Catholic Healthcare Commission. Bishop Field is a member of the National Executive of ACCORD and the Bishops' Commission on Healthcare/Disabilities/Drugs. He is also President of Pax Christi in Ireland.

Professor Patrick Hannon, a priest of the diocese of Cloyne, is an Emeritus Professor of Moral Theology at Maynooth. He holds doctorates in theology (Maynooth) and law (Cambridge) and is a member of the Irish Bar. He is a former chairman of the Irish Commission for Justice and Peace and of the Irish Commission for Prisoners Overseas. His most recent monograph is *Moral Decision Making* (Veritas, 2006).

Professor Ray Kinsella is on the faculty of the UCD Smurfit School and the Management Institute of Paris. He was awarded a Ph.D. in the field of Competition in Banking and subsequently studied at the IMF Institute in Washington DC. He was an Economist in the Central Bank and has held a number of senior academic posts. He has been a member of the Higher Education Authority (HEA), the Northern Ireland Economic Council, and is Visiting Professor at the Institute of European Finance. He is currently a member of the ICJSA. Professor Kinsella has researched, taught and published extensively on market structure and regulation in financial institutions and markets.

Dr Nuala O'Loan is the Police Ombudsman for Northern Ireland, responsible for the investigation of all complaints against the police. She is a qualified solicitor and was the Senior Lecturer holding the Jean Monnet Chair in European Law at the University of Ulster. She has produced more than fifty articles and other publications on law, policing, faith and other issues. For sixteen years she was a voluntary marriage counsellor. She is married and has five sons.

Dr Diarmuid Martin is Archbishop of Dublin and Primate of Ireland. He was ordained to the priesthood in 1969. He entered the service of the Holy See in 1976 in the Pontifical Council for the Family. In 1986 he was appointed Under-Secretary of the Pontifical Council of Justice and Peace, and in 1994 Secretary of the same Pontifical Council. In December 1998 he was appointed Titular Bishop of Glendalough and received the episcopal ordination on 6 January 1999. In March 2001 he was elevated to the rank of Archbishop and undertook responsibilities as Permanent Observer of the Holy See in Geneva, at the United Nations Office and Specialised Agencies and at the World Trade Organisation. He was appointed Coadjutor Archbishop of Dublin in May 2003, and was installed as Archbishop of Dublin on 26 April 2004. Archbishop Martin is Vice-President of the Irish Bishops' Conference, Chairman of its Department of Social Issues and International Affairs, Chairman of its Commission on Europe and a Trustee of Trócaire.

His Eminence Renato Raffaele Cardinal Martino is President of the Pontifical Council for Justice and Peace. Born in Salerno, Italy, he holds a doctorate in canon law and is fluent in French, Spanish, English and Portuguese. After finishing his studies, he entered the Vatican's Diplomatic Service in 1962, serving in Nicaragua, the Philippines, Lebanon and Brazil. In 1980 he was appointed as Apostolic Pro-Nuncio to Thailand,

Singapore, Laos and Malaysia. That same year he was ordained Titular Archbishop of Segermes. In 1983 he was appointed Apostolic Delegate to Brunei Darussalam. In 1986 he was appointed Permanent Observer of the Holy See to the United Nations, New York. In October 2002 he was appointed President of the Pontifical Council for Justice and Peace and was elevated to the College of Cardinals in October 2003.

John Murray graduated from Mater Dei Institute of Education, Dublin in 1985 and spent the next seventeen years teaching religion in second level schools in Ireland. In 2002, he began lecturing in Moral Theology at Mater Dei. He is the author of *Issues of Justice and Peace* (Veritas, 2005), one of the books in the *Into the Classroom* series accompanying the new Senior Cycle Syllabus in Religious Education. John and his wife and family live in Dublin.

Lord Chris Patten of Barnes is one of Britain's most respected political figures. He was appointed Chairman of the Conservative Party in 1990 and was made Governor of Hong Kong in 1992, a position he held until 1997 when he oversaw the return of Hong Kong to China. When he returned from his post, he became Chairman of the Independent Commission on Policing in Northern Ireland and was associated with the implementation of the Belfast Peace Agreement of 1998–1999. In September 1999 he was appointed European Commissioner for External Relations, and on leaving office in Brussels in 2004 was made a life peer.

Joan Roddy dmj has been Director of the Refugee and Migrant Project since it was set up by the Irish Bishops' Conference in 1999. Prior to that, she was involved with her congregation in several African countries, including Ghana, where for eight years she was part of a community development team. Earlier, she worked for almost a decade with the Kilkenny Social Services.

Sylvia Thompson is Chairperson of the Kerry Diocesan Justice, Peace and Creation Committee (partner of Pax Christi International). She is originally from Co. Limerick and has been living in Co. Kerry since 1994. She has been a member of Pax Christi since 1971 at local, national and international levels. In 1998/1999 Sylvia was invited onto the newly forming Kerry Diocesan Justice Committee, now the Kerry Diocesan Justice, Peace and Creation Committee. She works as a Speech and Language Therapist with Enable Ireland, and is based in Tralee.

FOREWORD

Bishop Raymond Field

The Compendium of the Social Doctrine of the Church was launched in Rome in October 2004 by His Eminence Cardinal Martino. I had the pleasure to be present along with Fr Tim Bartlett, Executive Secretary, Irish Commission for Justice and Social Affairs (ICJSA) at that significant event. It was decided then that as a Commission we should proceed as quickly as possible to have the *Compendium* published here in Ireland. In June 2005 it was presented by Archbishop Seán Brady and Archbishop Diarmuid Martin at a special celebration in Maynooth. I am grateful to Veritas for their support in achieving this task. I thank them along with Trócaire and the Knights of Columbanus for their sponsorship of this important event.

The social teaching of the Church is an essential part of the Christian message. At the same time we realise that we live in a broken world – a world which we Christians are constantly called on to renew. There are many issues at home and abroad on which we raise our concerns. We live in an unequal world. Over half the world's population of six billion people live in absolute poverty on less than $2 a day and must struggle with diseases while denied access to basic medicines so readily available in the west. Many suffer from a lack of food and a denial of basic human rights. Each year over 15,000 people die as a result of landmines. Over 300,000 children fight the wars of adults as child soldiers. Here at home, we are called to welcome the strangers amongst us, to welcome 'new Irish' who come to our country seeking employment and to build a life here. We see the gap between the rich and the poor grow wider as the more vulnerable are susceptible to relative poverty in our increasingly globalised economy. The Church's social doctrine calls above all on lay Christians everywhere to live in a society as a witness to Jesus Christ and to the Good News proclaimed in the Gospels.

Our objective at this Conference was twofold: to raise awareness of and to promote the social doctrine of the Church. It is in that context we wish to facilitate and encourage a conversation around many of the social issues which challenge us both nationally and internationally. To help achieve this we invited a distinguished group of speakers and guests from across a wide spectrum of our society, including senior public representatives, academics and business people, members of the media, public servants, church personnel and others involved in areas of social concern. Our speakers included An Taoiseach Bertie Ahern, Archbishop Diarmuid Martin, Professors William Binchy and Ray Kinsella, Mr David Begg, General Secretary, ICTU, Nuala O'Loan, Police Ombudsman for Northern Ireland, Ms Sylvia Thompson of the Kerry Diocesan Justice, Peace and Creation Committee, Sr Joan Roddy, Director, Refugee and Migrant Project, and Ms Deirdre Carroll, CEO of Inclusion Ireland. In addition, we were privileged to have speakers from abroad – His Eminence Cardinal Renato Raffaele Martino, President of the Pontifical Council for Justice and Peace, and Lord Chris Patten, one of Britains's most respected political figures.

We are deeply conscious too that all our work is inspired by the teachings of the Gospel. Since the launch of the Irish Commission for Justice and Social Affairs in 2005 quite an amount has been achieved in promoting the Social Gospel. I would like to express my thanks to the members of the ICJSA for their support and cooperation and for giving so much of their valuable expertise and time.

Bishop Raymond Field, DD
Chairman
Irish Commission for Justice and Social Affairs

INTRODUCTION

VALUES ON THE ISLAND OF IRELAND: Towards a Civilization of Love

Eoin G. Cassidy

One of the most remarkable aspects of the *Compendium of the Social Doctrine of the Church* is the manner in which it situates the social gospel in the context of what it describes as the fostering of a civilization of love. In this context, it proclaims that 'human relationships cannot be governed solely according to the measure of justice – only a humanity in which there reigns the civilization of love will be able to enjoy authentic and lasting peace' (583). The challenge is to translate that ideal into the lived social, cultural and economic realities of the world in which we live.

An introduction to a commentary on the *Compendium* that has its origins in an Irish context suggests the value of a brief reflection on the social and cultural mores of twenty-first century Ireland from the perspective of this ideal of a civilization of love. Given the different political, religious and economic realities that pertain north and south of the border, it may seem slightly artificial to attempt such an analysis. However, thanks to the findings of a study commissioned by the Economic and Social Research Institute (ESRI) in Dublin and based on the European Values Study (2000) this may not be the case.[1] What the authors found was compelling evidence that in terms of core values, Northern Irish Protestants and Catholics share much more with their southern counterparts than they do with the rest of the UK. Furthermore, these core values are not replicated to the same extent in any other country or region on the continent of Europe. This is particularly evident in the broad area of family and sexual morality where the differences between Northern Ireland and the Republic across all religions were very slight and, with few exceptions, they placed Ireland (North and South) at the conservative end of the scale of all European countries.[2] Similarly, on the question of socio-economic preferences, the 2000 European Values Study [EVS] survey place both the Republic and Northern Ireland side by side in a right of centre position *vis-à-vis* the rest of Europe.

> In both the North and the Republic, people lean towards individual rather than state responsibility for providing for people, towards greater competition, towards more freedom for firms from state control, towards greater incentive for individual effort rather than equalisation of incomes ...[3]

Finally, differences that presume a distinctive 'Protestant work ethic' or a North–South divide in relation to values and attitudes connected with work are seen to be illusory.[4]
To anyone who has lived through the Ireland of the 1980s the economic transformation of the Republic, described colloquially as the Celtic Tiger, has been remarkable. As recently as twenty years ago the southern Irish landscape was marked by levels of poverty, unemployment and emigration that had few parallels in the industrialised world. Currently, long-term poverty and unemployment levels are at historic lows, and even by the most conservative estimates the Republic of Ireland has a per capita income that is well above the OECD (Organisation for Economic Cooperation and Development) average.[5] Furthermore, emigration has been replaced by immigration levels that are unmatched by any of our European neighbours. According to the recently published 2006 census statistics[6] no less than 10% (419,733) of Irish are foreign-born, including 150,000 migrants from outside of the EU.

Given the legacy of a thirty year conflict, it is to be expected that the economic performance of Northern Ireland would not replicate that of the Republic. Nevertheless, there is evidence that, with the advent of the peace process and the recent restoration of devolved government, economic activity has begun to improve significantly. This is reflected in the increase in the number of migrants working in Northern Ireland and the low unemployment figures that have remained in the 4.1–4.6% range over the past year.[7] These unemployment figures are comparable with those in the Republic and substantially better than in the rest of the UK or in the EU.

It would seem evident that Ireland, both north and south, has in recent years become an attractive place to live and earn a livelihood but the extent to which this is replicated in the social and cultural landscape of contemporary Ireland is less clear. The importance that citizens attach to values associated with the tasks of combating disadvantage, promoting social solidarity and respecting persons and property in the core areas of the economy, justice, education and health either contribute to or hinder the establishment of a civilization of love.

There is a perception that as wealth increases social capital decreases and an examination of some of the Irish statistics might give credence to this belief. For example, growing material prosperity does not seem to have freed people to any great extent to engage in voluntary work on behalf of the community. The latest evidence is that only 20% of adults in the Republic are engaged in such work.[8] Furthermore, despite the unparalleled growth in the economy and the continuance of social partnership, the government in the Republic has yet to seriously tackle the issues that contribute to some of the highest levels of inequality in the OECD.[9] Based on the figure for the UK, inequality levels in Northern Ireland are only marginally better than in the Republic.

Recent crime statistics which highlight the high level of violent crime in the North and the steep rise in the number of recorded homicides in the South also serve to sound a note of caution against an all too positive evaluation of the social mores of Irish society.[10] Whereas, in the recent past, much of this crime in the North was attributable to the legacy of the conflict, there is evidence, both north and south, that such crime is increasingly drug related. The picture however is not all one-sided because the incidence of total recorded crime in the Republic has not seen any noticeable increase in the past ten to fifteen years. Furthermore, crime rates in the Republic remain low by European standards.[11] Whereas the incidence of recorded crime in Northern Ireland remains higher than in the Republic, nevertheless it is both lower than in other regions of the UK and has fallen in each of the past six years.[12]

In the area of education there is evidence of considerable progress both north and south of the border in combating educational disadvantage. In the early 1990s functional illiteracy levels among adults in both jurisdictions was higher than the European average. Progress has been made in countering this phenomenon by promoting higher participation rates in education. Currently in Northern Ireland the figure of 86.6% for the participation of 16- and 17-year-olds in full-time education compares favourably with the figure of 77.4% for the rest of the UK.[13] The comparable figure in the Republic for Leaving Certificate completion is 85.3%.[14] Despite considerable increases in funding however, spending on primary and post-primary education in the Republic remains below the OECD average and class size averages of twenty-four for primary-school pupils in the Republic is the second highest in the EU after the UK.[15] At the other end of the educational spectrum numbers in third level education in the Republic have increased by 50% in the past ten years.[16]

Despite public perception, healthcare provision in the Republic has improved significantly in the last ten years across all categories as measured in terms of death rates and life expectancy.[17] Substantial increases in funding over the past decade have helped to reverse the effects of earlier cutbacks and to bring the health budget up to the OECD average.[18] However, unlike Northern Ireland, issues surrounding the equity of access to healthcare in the Republic remain and there is little to indicate that projects currently in development will significantly address this issue.

Few would argue that the family is the bedrock of any coherent concept of a civilization of love. How healthy is the family in twenty-first-century Ireland? Leaving aside the transformation in attitudes to sexual morality that has occurred in Ireland (north and south) over the past twenty years, it is the changes in the relationship between parents and children – the emergence of a generational gulf to replace the generational gap – that is most commented upon. Both parents working away from home with increasingly long commutes brings with it a whole range of formal care arrangement for children outside of the family environment.[19] This is compounded by the fact that upwards of 12% of all children in the Republic are living in one-parent families. Furthermore, the culture is one in which children have the affluence, the space and the technology to create their own virtual families from among their peer groups and where the family meal is frequently a quick pit stop with the kitchen as a type of fast food outlet.

However one might assess the current state of the family in Ireland today, what is striking is the importance which Irish people (north and south) attach to the family and family values. Although Ireland has increasingly adopted more 'liberal' stances in the broad area of sexual morality, nevertheless, as recently as the year 2000, 90% of the population, both north and south, Catholic and Protestant, rated the family as very important in their lives and a similar proportion consider that 'more emphasis on family life' would be a good thing for the future. Not only are the Irish markedly more pro-family than most of their European neighbours but also no other broad domain of life is accorded such a degree of importance.[20] The commitment to the importance of the family can also be seen in the divorce figures both north and south which remain low by European standards. Furthermore, even with regard to work place practices in the Republic the situation is not as anti-family as might be supposed. What is not often adverted to is that the increase in full-time employment over the past ten years has been matched by an almost identical increase in part-time work – the adoption of family friendly work practices. The percentage of the workforce engaged in part-time work has increased by more than 50% in the ten years to 2004.[21]

Looking at the current Irish (north and south) social and cultural profile through the lens of recent surveys there is some evidence of a decline in the adherence to Christian values in the broad area of sexual ethics. Clearly there are socio-economic factors at work that contribute to this new environment. These would include the changing demographic, economic and work patterns in contemporary Ireland and the increasingly pluralist moral environment in which Irish people live. Furthermore, one should not underestimate the influence of the consumerist ethos of contemporary society. Increasingly it is the pragmatism of a consumerist world view which provides the lens through which all relationships are viewed and such an environment is not conducive to the promotion of an ideal such as life-long fidelity.[22]

One should not however exaggerate the extent to which Ireland has embraced this consumerist ethos. On the contrary, the importance that Irish people continue to attach to their local community and their sensitivity to the challenges posed by global poverty and inequity suggest a continuing commitment to the core social character of Christian living. As an instance of a commitment to these values one can point to the high level of support for Irish aid agencies, many of whom are religiously motivated. Contributions to those agencies working in the 'third world' has increased substantially over the past ten years, and the same can be said for government aid from the Republic which is scheduled to reach the UN goal of .7% of GDP by 2012. Furthermore, recent surveys point to the high level of acceptance in the Republic of the migrant community – the new Irish. Although there are examples of racist behaviour, the incidence of racism in the Republic is nevertheless considerably less than in other EU countries.[23]

Unfortunately, this is not the case in Northern Ireland where racism has been and continues to be a major problem. As recently as the year ending 31 March 2006 there was an increase of 15% in racist incidents which were reported to the PSNI.[24]

Review of papers

This publication emerged from a conference on the *Compendium of the Social Doctrine of the Church* on the theme of 'The Common Good in an Unequal World'. Section One, entitled 'Theological and Philosophical Reflections', consists of a number of papers that reflect on the underlying presuppositions of the *Compendium*. In a chapter entitled 'Towards a Civilization of Love' Cardinal Renato Raffaele Martino focuses upon the perspective of the building of the civilization of love and shows how this ideal can act as an interpretative key to the whole document. In a chapter entitled 'Justice Tempered by Love' Patrick Hannon challenges the notion that teaching about social justice is peripheral to the Church's mission. In a reflective comment, he concludes, 'For the Church, charity is not a kind of welfare activity which could equally well be left to others, but is a part of her nature, an indispensable expression of her very being'. In a chapter entitled 'Catholic Social Teaching: A Global Ethic' I reflect on the universal significance of Catholic social teaching and the challenges to that teaching posed by contemporary culture.

Section Two is entitled 'Faith and Politics'. It contains a number of papers that reflect on the complex relationship between Church and State and the role of Church social teaching in the public sphere. In a chapter entitled 'Christ and Caesar: Reflections on Faith and Politics in the *Compendium*' John Murray opens with a provocative rhetorical quotation from one of the early Church Fathers, Tertullian: 'What has Jerusalem to do with Athens?' His article explores the relationship between faith and politics in the *Compendium*, highlighting the manner in which it traces a delicate balance between the extremes of an exclusive monastic detachment from the world and an exclusively social activist standpoint. In a chapter entitled 'The Common Good in an Unequal World' An Taoiseach Bertie Ahern reflects on the nature of good governance and the wisdom that is to be gleaned from the social teaching of the Catholic Church. In a chapter entitled 'Thoughts on the *Compendium*: Challenges of the Twenty-First Century' Lord Chris Patten highlights a number of key cultural and political challenges facing the Church. Changes in the make-up of the family, the rise of a globalised economy, how to preserve the environment, the global commons and how to reshape our relationship with Islam for the common good all pose challenges and provide opportunities for the proclamation of the social gospel.

Section Three is entitled 'Solidarity and Freedom'. In this section, issues that give expression to the core 'left–right' debate in political theory are explored. In a chapter entitled 'A Shared Humanism based on Solidarity' Archbishop Diarmuid Martin observes that whereas the Church recognises the legitimate autonomy of the secular order of the human sciences it does not abandon its role in contributing to building a just social and civil order. In the course of his paper he highlights as the fundamental principle of any policy on social advancement that of 'enhancing human capacity'. It is a principle that respects the vision of human beings as subjects rather than objects of social policy. In 'Solidarity and Freedom: Defending the Rights and Dignity of Work in a Global Economy' David Begg reflects on the values that the *Compendium* espouses as it addresses the delicate issue of the relation between labour and capital. In a wide-ranging article that explores the challenges facing those who seek to uphold the dignity of work he acknowledges the importance of Catholic social teaching. In a chapter entitled 'Morality and the Market' Ray Kinsella acknowledges that 'the *Compendium* provides an alternative values-based vision of the future of the new *globalised* economic and environmental paradigm'. In the course of his paper Kinsella explores the relation between the market and morality from the perspective of the primacy of the person.

Section Four is entitled 'Rights and Responsibilities'. In this section, the authors explore the manner in which the *Compendium* challenges not only society but also the Church to work to ensure that core rights find concrete expression in today's world. In a chapter entitled 'Rights and Responsibilities' William Binchy addresses four key issues that have shaped human rights discourse. In the course of his paper he acknowledges that 'the central values of contemporary human rights theory on social justice are to be found in the *Compendium*'. In 'Disability and Difference' Deirdre Carroll argues forcibly for a new UN Convention on the rights of disabled people. She makes the point that the unambiguous statements in the *Compendium*, on the fundamental right of all people with disabilities to participate to the full in the economic, social and cultural life of their communities will strengthen this struggle. In a chapter entitled 'The Privatisation of Public Morality', Nuala O'Loan acknowledges the importance of the *Compendium* which gives a ready access to the articulation of the teaching of the Church in terms of social doctrine. In the course of a searching paper she raises questions about the manner in which the Church deals with those accused of crimes of sexual abuse. In a chapter entitled 'Global Movements of People' Joan Roddy quotes the Palestinian academic Edward Said who described exile as 'compelling to think about but terrible to experience'. Her paper provides compelling evidence that European laws on migration run counter to the importance that is attached to the family in the *Compendium*. In the final chapter in the book entitled 'Tilling the Garden', Sylvia Thompson offers a telling reminder of the ethical challenge posed by our relationship to the environment. There is an inescapable logic to the argument, the implications of which cannot be ignored.

Notes

1 Fahey, T., Hayes, B. and Sinnott, R., *Conflict and Consensus: A Study of Values and Attitudes in the Republic of Ireland and Northern Ireland*, Dublin, Institute of Public Administration, 2005.

2 Ibid., pp. 114–39. Interestingly, across all religions, the only significant differences recorded were between those of weak or no religious affiliation and those who are religious. The former expressed more liberal views in these areas.

3 Ibid., p. 145.

4 Ibid., p. 183.

5 The 2006 Republic of Ireland (ROI) GDP per capita figure is €42,771. Given the effect of multi-national companies GNI offers a more accurate measurement of Irish wealth. The 2006 GNI figure is €41,577.

6 Published on 28 June 2007.

7 Statistics issued by the Northern Ireland Executive dated 18 April 2007.

8 This Census 2006 figure of 20% is much lower than that collated from the 1999/2000 EVS figure of 33%. It is also much lower than the 2003 ESS [European Social Survey] which estimated that no less than 15% of adults contribute voluntarily to assisting sporting organisations (the 2006 census figure is of 180,465 adults engaged in voluntary work with a sporting organisation out of a total adult population of over three million). The only statistics for Northern Ireland are from the 2000 EVS survey which gives a figure of 21% – much lower than the comparable 33% for the Republic.

9 'It appears that rapid growth has not greatly affected the Irish ranking in terms of income inequality: the most recent figures suggest that Ireland [ROI] [and Northern Ireland as part of the UK] is in a quite large group of EU or OECD countries with a relatively high degree of economic inequality.' Brian Nolan and Bertrand Maitre, 'Economic Growth and Income Inequality: Setting the Context', in Fahey, T. et al. (eds) *Best of Times? The Social Impact of the Celtic Tiger*, Dublin, IPA, 2007, p. 41.

10 Between 1990 and 1992 the figures in the EU capital cities for homicides per million population residents placed Belfast (149.9) and Dublin (14.7) at opposite ends of the scale. The

figures for the period between 2000 and 2002 showed a dramatic decrease of approximately 50% in the figure for Belfast (62.4) and a similar increase in the figure for Dublin (21.2). Given these figures, the profile of Dublin is about average for EU capitals. The difference is that homicide rates have declined during this period in all of the EU capitals with the exception of Dublin.

11 The most recent comparative statistics on crime rates in the Republic are contained in Ian O'Donnell, 'Crime and its Consequences', *Best of Times?*, pp. 245–64.

12 Evidence for this can be found in the PSNI statistics on incidences of recorded crime in Northern Ireland.

13 Department of Education, Northern Ireland, statistics for the academic year 2005/2006.

14 Source: Department of Education (ROI) Annual Report for 2004.

15 Source: Central Statistics Office (CSO) 2006, Figures of 2004/05 cohort of Primary Pupils, Dublin, Stationery Office, p. 115. See also Dáil debate of 21 March 2007.

16 See Emer Smyth et al., 'Changing Times, Changing Schools? Quality of Life for Students', *Best of Times?*, pp. 139–54.

17 One of the areas generating most concern in the Republic is the phenomenon of young adult male suicides. At 20.4% (per 100,000) in the 20–24 age cohort, this figure is high by international standards. However, there is some evidence of a recent decline in this rate. See WHO suicide statistics. Recent data on suicides in Northern Ireland make for sobering reading. In an address to the Assembly (5 July 2007) the Minister for Health Michael McGimpsey announced that last year the number of those taking their own lives rose alarmingly to 291, nearly double the average recorded between 2000 and 2004. (Men under 35 years make up 40% of that figure.) Source: *Irish Times*, 6 July 2007.

18 See Richard Layte et al., 'Health and Health Care', *Best of Times?*, pp. 105–22.

19 An example of this phenomenon can be seen in the increase from 38.5% of women in full-time employment to 56.5% in the ten years up to 2004. See Philip O'Connell et al., 'Employment and the Quality of Work', *Best of Times?*, p. 45.

20 EVS Survey 2000. See Conflict and Consensus, pp. 118–21.

21 As of 2004 this figure stands at 16.8% of the working population – an increase from the 1993 figure of 10.5%. Source: CSO Labour Force and National Household Survey, 2004.

22 See Eoin G. Cassidy, 'Modernity and Religion in Ireland: 1980–2000' in Cassidy, E. (ed.) *Measuring Ireland: Discerning Values and Beliefs*, Dublin, Veritas, 2002, pp. 17–45.

23 See Gerard Hughes et al., 'The Impact of Immigration', *Best of Times?*, pp. 217–44.

24 Source: Belfast Telegraph, 16 October 2006. In a Northern Ireland Assembly debate on racial equality, 3 July 2007, the Sinn Féin spokesperson Martina Anderson claimed that the numbers of racist incidents continues to rise – 936 incidents in the past year, double the total for the previous two years. Source: *Irish Times*, 4 July 2007.

OPENING ADDRESS

Archbishop Seán Brady

It is most appropriate that this conference is held at the beginning of the season of Lent. As the ashes are placed on our foreheads, we are reminded that the Christian journey is one of continual transformation, of *metonoia*, of making all things new. The source and challenge of that transformation is both external and internal. It is of immense significance to all those who seek to be more than social engineers in the search for justice and peace that Jesus located the prospect of the civilization of love in a radical change of attitude – in the Beatitudes – the attitudes of the truly happy. As anyone who has sought to resolve conflict through threat of force or even legal agreement will know, as anyone who has sought to mobilise people to the concerns of the poor and hungry of our world will know, or as those who sought to engage societies of busy people in concern for the sustainability of our environment will know, the best thought-out policies, the most comprehensive agreements will all flounder without a fundamental change of attitude.

The Beatitudes touch on all of the great journeys of transformation and open for us the possibility and the vision of a civilization of love. At their heart, as our conference theme suggests, is 'the firm and persevering determination to commit oneself to the common good; that is, to the good of all and of each individual, because we are really responsible for all'. The Beatitudes remind us how quickly the legitimate pursuit of personal or national economic growth can become separated from its proper orientation towards the common good and from the principle of the universal destiny of the goods of the earth. There is ample evidence in our own society that the richer we get, the more inclined we are to think of compassion, aid and the selfless service of others as luxury items, things to be considered only when everything else is paid for and done.

This suggests, at least in part, that the shift to a more global consciousness has not yet been met with a shift towards a more global conscience, that we are still inclined to look after our own interests first, both as individuals and as nation states.

And this brings us back to our Lenten journey, to those simple ashes which remind us so publicly of our shared humanity, based on solidarity. As we gather today to reflect more intensely on the implications of that innate solidarity, let us ask the Lord to deepen our transformation and to help to make that civilization of love which he proclaimed a more transparent and tangible reality in our world and in all its dimensions.

SECTION ONE

Theological and Philosophical Reflections

1

TOWARDS A CIVILIZATION OF LOVE: The Challenge of Catholic Social Doctrine Today

Cardinal Renato Raffaele Martino

The conference on the *Compendium* is a significant undertaking that does honour to its organisers, for it is by means of such initiatives that we are able to make manifest in times that are so complex and difficult our willingness to deal with issues coming to us from the field of Christian social ethics. I make this presentation of the Compendium from the perspective of the building of the civilization of love. This perspective serves to highlight in a very evident manner the fundamental purpose of the Church's social doctrine, which is the building of a more human society. In fact, the first task to which this doctrine calls believers is that of spreading love in social relationships, at every level and in every area. Jesus teaches us that the 'fundamental law of human perfection, and consequently of the transformation of the world, is the new commandment of love' (cf. Mt 22:40; Jn 15:12; Col 3:14; Jas 2:8; *Compendium* 580, 103).[1] Only love can completely change man and society (cf. *Compendium*, 583).[2]

The *Compendium* has a simple and straightforward structure. After an introduction, there follows three parts. The first, composed of four chapters, deals with the fundamental presuppositions of social doctrine – God's plan of love for humanity and for society, the Church's mission and the nature of social doctrine, the human person and human rights, the principles and values of social doctrine. The second part, composed of seven chapters, deals with the contents and classical themes of social doctrine – the family, human work, economic life, the political community, the international community, the environment and peace. The third part – which is quite brief, being composed of one sole chapter – contains a series of indications for the use of social doctrine in the pastoral praxis of the Church and in the life of Christians, above all the lay faithful. The conclusion, entitled 'For a Civilization of Love', is an expression of the underlying purpose of the entire document.

The Compendium places social doctrine at the heart of the Church's mission. The Church – existing in the world and for the world, although not of the world – cannot neglect her mission of breathing Christian life into the world.[3] When the Church takes an interest in human promotion, when she proclaims the rules for a new coexistence in peace and justice, when she works with all people of good will for creating relations and institutions that are more human, she 'teaches the way which man must follow in this world in order to enter the Kingdom of God. Her teaching therefore extends to the whole moral order, and notably to the justice which must regulate human relations. This is part of the preaching of the Gospel'.[4] The fact that the *Compendium* places social doctrine within the proper mission of the Church, on the one hand, means that social doctrine must not be considered as something added on, as something incidental to Christian life; on the other hand, it is an aid in understanding how this doctrine belongs to a community subject. The adequate subject of social doctrine, in fact, is nothing other than the entire ecclesial community. In paragraph 79, the *Compendium* affirms:

> The social doctrine belongs to the Church because the Church is the subject that formulates it, disseminates it and teaches it. It is not a prerogative of a certain component of the ecclesial body but of the entire community; it is the expression of the way that the Church understands society and of her position regarding social structures and changes. The whole of

> the Church community – priests, religious and laity – participates in the formulation of this social doctrine, each according to the different tasks, charisms and ministries found within her.

The Compendium is put forward as a manifesto for bringing about a new humanism, in the perspective of the civilization of love. Presenting it in this way does not seem to involve a forced interpretation. In fact, in the introduction we find the statement that the *Compendium* has been drawn up in order to promote and sow the seeds for the civilization of an integral humanism in solidarity that is open to Transcendence (cf. 7). It is a *manifesto* in the sense that within it are found the indications – as they exist both in the mind and in history – of a new society, in order to give concrete expression to the ever-pressing requirements of the Gospel and of Christianity, so that they may dwell in the hearts of men and women. Humanity cannot live without prospects for the future, without some guiding principle. It is always necessary for the essence of Christianity to be translated into concrete terms, in every context and historical period. It is necessary for the riches of the Gospel to take on new life and to extend into the *social and cultural ethos of peoples*, so that every generation may have hope, so that the commitment of every generation to the growth of civilization may be strengthened. In the current context of globalisation, in fact, the *Compendium* traces out for the human family an integral humanism in solidarity and calls on all to make an investment in the best part of individuals and peoples, in the positive energies of history.

The *Compendium* is undoubtedly a complex and articulate text that does not allow us, in this context, to consider all its various themes in their vastness. Allow me, therefore, to make a few brief comments that may be of some usefulness and relevance.

Rediscovering the common good

If you leaf through the pages of the Analytical Index of the *Compendium*, you will see that the expression 'common good' is one of the most frequently occurring. It may sometimes seem, however, that this concept has been removed from the current agendas of economic and political life. Social doctrine continues to insist on it with force, describing its characteristics in the following words:

> The common good does not consist in the simple sum of the particular goods of each subject of a society entity. Belonging to everyone and to each person, it is and remains 'common', because it is indivisible and because only together is it possible to attain it, increase it and safeguard its effectiveness, with regard also to the future. Just as the moral actions of an individual are accomplished in doing what is good, so too the actions of a society attain their full stature when they bring about the common good. The common good, in fact, can be understood as the social and community dimension of the moral good. (164)

The Compendium has a vision of the common good that is above all subsidiary, in that the common good is to be pursued by fostering participation and the taking on of responsibility in a manner that makes full use of the *principle of subsidiarity*. This is a theme of great relevance. The *Compendium* states:

> The principle of subsidiarity protects people from abuses by higher-level social authority and calls on these same authorities to help individuals and intermediate groups to fulfil their duties. This principle is imperative because every person, family and intermediate group has something original to offer to the community. Experience shows that the denial of

> subsidiarity, or its limitation in the name of an alleged democratisation or equality of all members of society, limits and sometimes even destroys the spirit of freedom and initiative. (187)

Strengthening the relationship between ethics and the economy

In its approach to the economy, the *Compendium* forcefully emphasises the *relationship of ethics* (cf. 330–5). The economy and economic institutions occupy that dimension of the social–relational life of men and women that seeks, in a manner quantitatively and qualitatively appreciable, to meet the primary needs that arise as a consequence of people's existence in the world. Within this perspective is found the *intrinsically ethical dimension of the economy*, both as a practical aspect of human life and as a science. In fact, the human person is at the centre of economic quests and economic praxis, as has been repeated many times by the Church's social magisterium, which has even declared man as 'the source, the centre and the purpose of all economic and social life' (*Gaudium et spes*, 63). The economy has explicit needs of ethics, for both the economy and ethics find their foundation and their *raison d'être* in man; both of them seek, albeit from different perspectives, to understand man in all the fullness of his dignity.

It is within this perspective that we are to place the question, of great current interest and highly debated, of the value to be given to the market. Or, to be more precise, we may ask: what is said in the *Compendium* about the regulation of the market and about who should regulate the market? The *Compendium* tells us that the market must be regulated in the first place because it is not right that all goods should pass by way of the market. In the second place, because there are needs that the market is not able to satisfy. Third, because there are people who – due to situations of want into which they were born, to poverty or to losses suffered in life – are not able to gain access to necessary goods. Fourth, because there are goods that belong to everyone and that do well to remain the common property of all (cf. 347–50).

We come now to the second question: who must regulate the market? I believe that by now we are all convinced that the market must be regulated by different subjects. The market must first of all be regulated by its own rules. Transparency, knowledge, trust, lawful competition, economic democracy: these are first of all economic rules that have tremendous value and tremendous importance (cf. 348). Second, the market is regulated by the ethics of business owners and of those who work in the economic sector, because external rules have much less binding force than the rules internalised in the consciences of those active in the economic sector (cf. 343). Third, a people's culture and tradition contribute to regulating the market. This obviously includes religion. The market always exists within a culture; it does not exist in a pure state as a mere technical fact; social bonds of solidarity, models of behaviour are of vital importance for giving the market a soul. The ethics of work that come from the religious order, the ethics of sacrifice of so many business owners, family bonds: these are all phenomena with great weight in terms of providing ethical direction to economic activity (cf. no. 350). Fourth, the market is also regulated by legitimate divergences between the different sectors of society, by associations of people in various work categories and by labour unions that democratically demand respect for the rights of workers. Healthy clashes of social opinion have never been condemned by the Church, which, indeed, sees in them prospects for progress, provided that they never give rise to violent or ideological conflicts (cf. 306). Fifth, the market is regulated by civil society: by consumer associations, by education, by families, by public opinion. An important regulatory factor for the market, from the Church's perspective, is also represented by the non-profit economy of the so-called third sector, which is a full-fledged partner in the market, although it operates according to criteria not exclusively of efficiency, but also of solidarity (cf. 356–7). Last, economic organisations and international financial organisations are factors of regulation for the market when they succeed in their aim of providing the market with equitable rules, fostering economic democracy (cf. 370–2). All these factors together with the political authorities contribute to the regulation of the market (cf. 351–3).

As can readily be seen, the issue of the market is an issue of governance, that is, of dynamic and regulated orientation on the part of various subjects that must be integrated among themselves according to the principle of subsidiarity. I believe I can affirm that in our globalised era these factors are being imposed as if with new force and that the urgent need to coordinate them, with a view to an economic order ethically oriented to the service of the person, can no longer be avoided.

The political community and democracy

The *Compendium* states that the first contribution that the Church offers the political community is of a religious type and corresponds to her mission: preserving and promoting in the conscience of all the sense of the transcendent dignity of the human person. As declared in no. 26 of *Gaudium et spes*: 'The ferment of the Gospel too has aroused and continues to arouse in man's heart the irresistible requirements of his dignity.' In the message of Christ, the human community can find the strength that will enable people to love their neighbour as another self, to combat all that is contrary to life, to accept the fundamental equality of all, to fight against every form of discrimination, to overcome a purely individualistic ethic in the perspective of civil friendship (cf. 390–2).

In this perspective, religious freedom is a good for society. A secular autonomy that is truly autonomous would guarantee this religious freedom and permit the Church to undertake this task that has a public value, although it is not directly political. Making reference to *Gaudium et spes*, the *Compendium* specifies very well the proper function of the Church with regards to the political order:

> The Church is not to be confused with the political community and is not bound to any political system.[5] In fact, the political community and the Church are autonomous and independent of each other in their own fields, and both are, even if under different titles, 'devoted to the service of the personal and social vocation of the same human beings'.[6] Indeed, it can be affirmed that the distinction between religion and politics and the principle of religious freedom constitute a specific achievement of Christianity and one of its fundamental historical and cultural contributions. (50)

We can also affirm that the principle of secular autonomy and the principle of religious freedom represent a specific acquisition of Christianity, and an acquisition of great significance on the level of history and culture.

The *Compendium* speaks also of democracy, the political system that, better than any other, fosters participation and therefore mutual solidarity and cooperation within the political community. I would summarise the *Compendium* 's reflection on democracy in these terms: democracy is an instrument and not an end; nonetheless even if it is only an instrument it must not be reduced to mere procedure.

> An authentic democracy is not merely the result of a formal observation of a set of rules but is the fruit of a convinced acceptance of the values that inspire democratic procedures. (407)

For this reason, the *Compendium* understands and proposes democracy as a political system that allows for the protection and development of the person, understood as an unconditional reality. The Christian vision of the person is distinguished by the absolute character recognised in the person deriving from the fact of men and women being the *imago Dei*: this means that the human person cannot be reduced to something less, or be considered a means and not an end, or be understood in a partial and reductive sense. Indeed, this vision requires that the person be understood in his horizontal and vertical openness, and in his capacity to relate to others and to God in truth and goodness. A true democracy needs this humanist and personalist soul (cf. 407).

Living in harmony with nature

The *Compendium* speaks of this harmony, with balance and vision, in the chapter on safeguarding the environment. The key point put forth by the *Compendium* is the following: human action with regard to nature must be guided by ethics. The ecological problem must therefore be seen as an ethical problem, since there is a constant interaction between the human person and nature (cf. 461–5). But nature cannot be understood in an ethical sense if it is considered only from a point of view that idolatrises it, or if it is understood as a field for the indiscriminate exercise of technology. In the perspective of the *Compendium*, the ecological emergency is also an anthropological emergency. The way that we relate to the world depends on the way that mankind relates to itself. But we must also add that the way that man looks inside himself depends on how he turns to God. When man wishes to set himself up in the place of God he loses sight of himself and of his responsibility to govern nature (cf. 487).

Promoting peace

We can understand the *Compendium* 's reflection on peace if we make a distinction between peace as the absence of war and peace as life that is fully human. The *Compendium* is concerned many times with peace in the first sense, but it is concerned even more – infinitely more and constantly so – with peace in the second sense. This, in fact, is the 'fullness' of peace, which includes truth, freedom and justice, and which alone makes it possible to arrive firmly at peace as the absence of war. I do not believe I am in error in saying that the *Compendium* always speaks of peace, even when it does not use this word; it speaks of peace also when it speaks of justice or solidarity, of the unity of the human family, of God's plan for humanity, of the human rights of every person and the corresponding duties, of the dignity of the human person, peoples and cultures. In the *Compendium*, therefore, peace also takes on a powerful cultural significance that is very relevant for today. The sense of mutual respect for religious and cultural traditions, dialogue between religions, international cooperation, a culture of openness: these are all fundamental dimensions that foster peace. According to the *Compendium*, at play here is the ultimate meaning of the building up of human society and, consequently, of peace (cf. 494–6).

As I conclude, I wish to make a connection between the *Compendium* and the first encyclical letter of our Holy Father, Pope Benedict XVI. In fact, placed at the heart of *Deus caritas est* – especially in paragraphs 26–9 – is the Church's social doctrine, explicitly referred to also in paragraph 27 with the historical sketch from *Rerum Novarum* to *Centesimus annus*. In the same place, moreover, reference is made to the publication of the *Compendium of the Social Doctrine of the Church*, which has made a 'comprehensive presentation' of the entire social teaching of the Church. We can therefore say that the encyclical letter takes in not only certain aspects of social doctrine but the whole of the Church's modern social magisterium. Social doctrine is placed within – and not at the margins of – the Christian proclamation that *God is love*. Social doctrine, accordingly, is connected with the love that, as a theological virtue, is the divine life itself that nourishes the Church in her service to the world, and that, as a human virtue, is that civil and social friendship without which the community bonds between men grow weak and uncertain. *Deus caritas est* proclaims love as the very essence of God, and precisely for this reason it does not fail to consider the human and social aspects of love, which are illuminated and purified in that light. Within this dialogue between the divine and the human is found the social doctrine of the Church, which must continuously make appeals to that love that comes from divine life while at the same time it must bend down lovingly to the needs of humanity.

The connection between the Church's social doctrine and love is therefore very deep. This doctrine is at the service of the individual person known and loved in the fullness of his or her calling, and has as its purpose the care and responsibility for man whom Christ himself has entrusted to the Church. Moreover, the original connection between the Church's social doctrine and God's love – or God who is love – is found in the decisive and essential fact that this doctrine is the Church proclaiming 'the truth about Christ, about herself and about man' (*Sollicitudo rei socialis*, 41), and the heart of this proclamation is that God is love. It is no coincidence that the *Compendium of the Social Doctrine of the Church* begins with the first chapter entitled 'God's Plan of Love for Humanity' and ends with a conclusion entitled 'For a Civilization of Love'.

Notes

1 Second Vatican Council, Pastoral Constitution, *Gaudium et spes*, 28; cf. ibid., Dogmatic Constitution, *Lumen gentium*, 42; *Catechism of the Catholic Church*, 826.

2 Cf. John Paul II, Apostolic Letter, *Novo Millennio Ineunte*, 49–51.

3 'The Church has the right to be a teacher for mankind, a teacher of the truth of faith: the truth not only of dogmas but also of the morals whose source lies in human nature itself and in the Gospel ... This right of the Church is at the same time a duty, because she cannot forsake this responsibility without denying herself and her fidelity to Christ: "Woe to me if I do not preach the Gospel!" (1 Cor 9:16)' (*Compendium*, 70–1).

4 Congregation for the Doctrine of the Faith, Instruction, *Libertatis Conscientiae*, 63.

5 Cf. Second Vatican Council, Pastoral Constitution, *Gaudium et spes*, 76: AAS 58 (1966). 1099; cf. *Catechism of the Catholic Church*, 2245.

6 Second Vatican Council, Pastoral Constitution, *Gaudium et spes*, 76: AAS 58 (1966), 1099.

2

JUSTICE TEMPERED BY LOVE[1]

Patrick Hannon

A commonplace of commentary following the death of John Paul II was that though conservative on sexual morality he was progressive in his social teaching. Pope Benedict was expected to be no less conservative on sexual morality, but commentators evinced surprise at his positive appraisal of eros in *Deus caritas est*, even as they scanned the second part of the encyclical for evidence of a retrenchment on some of the positions on social justice which his predecessor had taken.

There is some truth in such generalisations and on the whole they are probably harmless, but they may mask preconceptions of a kind that can distort the Christian gospel. It is still possible to meet the view that morality is about sexuality and about nothing much else, and it is still possible to meet the view that 'social' teaching isn't really about morality at all. A related notion is that whereas sexual ethics are at the core of Christian moral doctrine, teaching about social justice is peripheral, and not at all to be taken as seriously. This latter becomes entangled sometimes with another question, that of the scope and binding character of official Catholic teaching. Students of Church–State relations in the Ireland of the 1950s may recall an attempt to discredit the Catholic bishops' approach to Dr Noel Browne's Mother and Child scheme by saying that it was 'only' social teaching, and therefore not binding on the consciences of politicians or people. And lest it be thought that this distinction was peculiar to a benighted

Ireland half a century ago, a glance at the debate surrounding the US Bishops' pastoral *Economic Justice for All* (1983) will indicate its persistence in a very different time and place.

There are reasons for these misconceptions and confusions, odd as they may now appear, and we shall be touching on some of them later. But it may as well be noted at the outset that there is no Christian warrant for minimising the place of social responsibilities, the 'social vocation', the mutual responsibilities of community and members, and the responsibilities also *vis-à-vis* the lesser communities of which we are each also a part. A pietist or quietist spirituality which would have members withdraw from engagement with the challenges of living in today's world is one form of Christian spirituality but it is not the only form, nor by itself could it suffice as witness to the riches of the Gospel message.

One has only to remember the beginning of Jesus' public ministry as told by Luke: he reads in the synagogue a prophecy of Isaiah which speaks of an anointing by the Spirit of the Lord which confers a mission to bring good news to the poor, proclaim release to the captive, sight to the blind, and freedom from oppression; and he tells them that on this day that prophecy is being fulfilled. There is a place for contemplation, even – indeed especially – for one who is living a life of active apostolate in the world, and Jesus provides an example in this regard. But an emphasis on the need for contemplation should not seek to devalue commitment to the Church's work of justice and of peace.

The fact remains that for a variety of reasons this dimension of gospel witness was not always or sufficiently honoured, though we needn't here take time over what it is anachronistic to bewail. For reasons to do with the kind of books they were – textbooks for training future priests for the work of the confessional – the manuals of moral theology in use from the beginning of the seventeenth century to the middle of the twentieth dealt with questions of justice largely in terms of individual and interpersonal justice, and matters of 'distributive' and 'legal' justice, as social justice was called, were treated only briefly if at all. Even after social justice became a theme of papal teaching it took some time before it began to be regarded as a standard item in Catholic moral theology. A standard item it is now though, and the scope of the term has broadened to include not just the ethics of the interrelationships of individual and society but also the interrelationships of individual and society with the *societies* of which the larger society is constituted – marriage, family, the world of work, and so on. Indeed, as a glance at the *Compendium* shows, Catholic social teaching is now concerned with nothing less than the entire canvas of human social relationships.

The corpus to which the name 'social teaching' is given has its origin in an encyclical of Leo XIII, *Rerum Novarum*, published in 1891, and the term is associated in a special way with the magisterium of the popes since then. But it is worth noting that vital contributions have been made by the Second Vatican Council, by a Synod of the world's bishops in 1971, by local and regional episcopal teaching bodies, and by the permanent secretariat of the Pontifical Council for Justice and Peace which is responsible for the *Compendium*. Nor should it be forgotten that Catholic social thought is continually enriched by the witness of praxis throughout the world.[2]

That a distinctive social doctrine began to evolve during the papacy of Leo XIII was a consequence of great societal change in Europe during the nineteenth century, and at the centre of this change was what we now call the Industrial Revolution. For this bespoke new social realities and unprecedented social problems, as crowds of men, women and children came to live and work in towns and cities, and as the question of the value and circumstances of their labour as well as the necessities of their livelihood came into view against a background of capitalist economics. A second key factor was the rise of the nation states and of liberal democratic forms of government. How was government to promote social order in the changed situation, how ensure just distribution of property and the new wealth, how safeguard and enhance the conditions for a true human fulfilment for all people of every class? And – a different type of question but plainly also critical – how ensure participation in the new political systems, so that peoples could truly govern themselves?

It is usual to observe that a constructive Catholic answer to these and related questions was late in coming, and that is true if we are thinking only of the emergence with Leo XIII of a papal social teaching which began to stand as an official challenge to the way in which employers were treating workers, and to the conditions in which so many were expected to live their lives. But this is to forget a different kind of witness to gospel values which long predated the encyclical: the care for the poor and the sick that was the mission of so many orders and congregations of women and men, not to mention the work of lay movements like Frederic Ozanam's St Vincent de Paul Society.

It remains true that Church leaders had been wary of political ideas associated with the revolutions of the late eighteenth and the nineteenth centuries, and in particular they had been opposed to anything that appeared to savour 'socialism'. Pope Leo and several of his successors were at pains to make it clear that there was a right to private property, and indeed that right is still affirmed in Catholic teaching. Limitations as to its exercise, clearly evident in patristic and scholastic thinking, were not in the forefront of Leo's mind, but they are intimated more and more clearly in each of the social encyclicals since his time. Church leaders had been wary too of the notion of human rights, in part again because of its association with political philosophies and revolutionary movements which targeted religion and Church as well as aristocracies. Leo, even if cautiously, overcame the suspicion attendant on 'rights talk', insisting on the entitlement of workers to a just wage, to decent working conditions and to association for the promotion and defence of their rightful interests. With the papacy of John XXIII the Church's magisterium was making free use of the concepts and devices of human rights discourse, and this way of thinking and talking about morality is now characteristic of Catholic social thought.

What we have seen in the hundred and twenty or so years since Leo's encyclical then is the incremental development of a body of official Catholic teaching which addresses the life of today's man and woman in today's world. That life and our world are full of complexity, and so the teaching is complex. And yet its essence lies in a few ideas which may be simply enough expressed. For in its essence it is only an elaboration of the call of Jesus that we should have love, one for another. Easier said than done of course, and it is not always easy to know what love requires. But a starting-point in Catholic social thought is that each human being is made in the image of God, so that each possesses an intrinsic dignity, and we each possess it equally. And that dignity calls for acknowledgment, and acknowledgement means giving people what is their due, and in the first place what is their due by virtue simply of being human. What *that* is, spelled out, may be found in any modern standard enumeration of human rights, following the first international instrument, the UN Declaration on Human Rights of 1948. And the extent to which Catholic social teaching makes the content of these enumerations its own may be seen from a reading of the *Compendium*.

So the demands of the commandment that we should have love, one for another, may be specified in terms of regard for human rights, even if such (or any) specification cannot capture in full the meaning of *agape*. And it is plain that these rights have to be protected and promoted and defended; and that, human nature being what it is, there is necessarily a role for law and the institutions of state; and indeed that some rights can be assured of implementation only through the mechanisms of government and law.

But Catholic social teaching is not confined to an endorsement of the entitlements that have come to be recognised as human rights; nor does it purport to say how every right is concretely to be implemented. What it does is to offer a vision of the human in the light of which human rights and responsibilities may be understood. The vision includes transcendence, as to human origins and identity and destiny; and it transforms and illuminates, so that, sin notwithstanding, what is created is also seen as graced.

The view of human rights offered by this teaching is not visionary only, and there is much that is concrete and practical – about citizenship, the family, political life, international relations, about the realities of life lived in the *polis* in our time. A controlling idea, put negatively, is that it seeks to avoid the excesses of both an individualistic and a collectivist approach. More positively, there are characteristic emphases, having indeed the force of principles, whose intent is to this effect. The most basic of these is the teaching's insistence on the importance of having regard to the 'common good'. This expression, and to some extent the idea, has an ancient pedigree in Graeco-Roman philosophy and is found in the writings of the medieval scholastic theologians, notably St Thomas Aquinas. Similar expressions – common welfare, for example, or common weal, or commonwealth – can be found in more modern philosophies, as can alternatives such as public good, public welfare and the like. And of course the term has latterly become part of the rhetoric of democratic politics in many countries of the world. But the notion of a common good, contrasted with individual or personal good, has been understood differently at different times and by different users of the term, and even in Catholic social teaching there are tensions in concept and usage that can be perplexing. Yet it is possible to identify some persistent themes in the teaching and, following the account found in the *Catechism of the Catholic Church*, it is possible to present in systematic form the main lines of a Catholic understanding of the common good.

The core insight is that the human person is a social or relational or community being; and this is not just because we need others for the necessities of survival but because we flourish only in the measure in which the person transcends self in love. The good of every person is found in community with others, and there is a common good – better perhaps, common good*s* – which are the context and accompaniment of the fulfillment of each. And so, in a phrase from Vatican II's *Gaudium et spes* which echoes Pope John XXIII's *Mater et magistra,* the *Catechism* declares that the common good is 'the sum of those conditions of social life which allow both social groups and their individual members relatively thorough and ready access to their own fulfillment'. This is of course a quite general description; one must ask, what are these conditions? The *Catechism* sets them out in summary form in terms of 'three essential elements'. First, there are 'the fundamental and inalienable rights of the human person', among which explicit mention is made of the right to follow conscience. Second, the common good requires 'the social well-being and development of the group itself'; and the civil authority 'should make accessible to each what is needed to lead a truly human life: food, clothing, health, work, education and culture, suitable information, the right to establish a family, and so on.' Third, the common good requires peace, 'that is, the stability and security of a just order'.

It was suggested above that one might speak of common goods, and this is because, as the *Catechism* puts it, 'each human community possesses a common good which permits it to be recognised as such'. Catholic social teaching in general makes special mention of 'intermediate' communities – those groupings other than the political community of which the person may also be a member. But 'it is in the political community that its [the common good] most complete realisation is found'. And 'it is the role of the state to defend and promote the common good of civil society, its citizens, and intermediate bodies'. But there is a further dimension of the common good which has been disclosing itself in our times, the *Catechism* notes: 'Human interdependence is increasing and gradually spreading throughout the world. The unity of the human family, embracing people who enjoy equal natural dignity, implies a universal common good.' And this good requires 'an organisation of the community of nations' which will be able to provide for the different needs of people, including food, hygiene, education, seeking in particular to alleviate the miseries of refugees throughout the world, and assisting migrants and their families.

An insistence on the common good or common goods is clearly a counterbalance to individualism. But it is important to hold in mind that, as is plain from the foregoing, in Catholic social thought the common good is nevertheless not something *over against* individual freedom; rather is the individual's freedom a part of the common good? Nor is the common good the aggregate of individual goods, or the good of a majority society. It is instructive to recall that the common good was a theme of writers such as Jacques Maritain who were as opposed to totalitarianisms of the right and left as much as to unbridled individualism.

A second key emphasis in Catholic social teaching is what is somewhat cumbersomely called the universal destination of goods, and what it means is put plainly in words from the Second Vatican Council's *Gaudium et spes*: 'God destined the earth and all it contains for all men and all peoples so that all created things would be shared fairly by all mankind under the guidance of justice tempered by charity.' This is, says the *Compendium*, a natural right, innate and antecedent to all positive law, so that, as Paul VI in *Populorum progressio* expressed it:

> All other rights, whatever they are, including property rights and the right of free trade, must be subordinated to this norm; they must not hinder it, but must rather expedite its application. It must be considered a serious and urgent social obligation to refer these rights to their original purpose.

A third characteristic emphasis is on human solidarity. The term inevitably evokes memories of the Polish trade union led by Lech Walesa, and also of Pope John Paul II in whose political and social philosophy it had a key role. But as used in magisterial teaching the idea goes back to an early stage in the development of Catholic social thought, and it was associated especially with the influential work of the German Jesuit Heinrich Pesch, whose student Oswald von Nell-Breuning was centrally involved in drafting Pius XI's *Quadragesimo anno*. The terms refer in the first place to the factual interdependence of human beings, an interdependence that in our world is found at all levels, and indeed includes the mutual relationships of human and other life that are the concern of ecology. Human beings are inherently social, cannot come to be or to grow, apart from relationships of many and varied kinds. The solidarity thus engendered needs to be acknowledged and respected: there needs to be a *sense* of our solidarity with humankind and with the rest of creation, which will include a sense of our *responsibility* for each other and for our world.

The *Compendium* puts the moral challenge in clear terms:

> In the presence of the phenomenon of interdependence and its constant expansion ... there persist in every part of the world stark inequalities between developed and developing countries, inequalities stoked also by various forms of exploitation, oppression and corruption that have a negative influence on the internal and international life of many states. The acceleration of interdependence between persons and peoples needs to be accompanied by equally intense efforts on the ethical–social plane, in order to avoid the dangerous consequences of perpetrating injustice on a global scale. (192)

A commitment to solidarity 'translates into the willingness to give oneself for the good of one's neighbour, beyond any individual or particular interest'.

A fourth emphasis is one that has achieved currency even in secular social thought, that known as the principle of subsidiarity. *Subsidium* is a Latin word for help or support, and at one level the principle refers to the fact that individuals and social groups require for their development the support of entities that are, so to speak, 'above' them. Thus, in order to flourish, a person ordinarily needs the help of the family, which in turn needs various kinds of support from the wider community, including the support of its political and social institutions, including the state. Looked at in this way, the principle of subsidiarity draws attention to the responsibilities that a society has to help its members achieve their potential in fullest measure.

But an equally important aspect of the principle is that a higher body should not take over what can be done by a lower. The *Compendium* quotes *Quadragesimo anno*:

> Just as it is gravely wrong to take from individuals what they can accomplish by their own initiative and industry and give it to the community, so also it is an injustice and at the same time a grave evil and disturbance of right order to assign to a greater and higher association what lesser and subordinate organisations can do. For every social activity ought of its very nature to furnish help to the members of the body social, and never destroy and absorb them. (186 [399])

The principle of subsidiarity is generally acknowledged to be one of the most valuable contributions of Roman Catholicism to modern socio-political thought. At first its scope was confined to intra-state political and social activity, but in time, and decisively in the social encyclicals of John XXIII, Paul VI and John Paul II, it was taken to apply also to international relations. Probably the best-known application of the idea in a wider context in modern Europe is its adoption as a principle of the law of the European Union.

A fifth principle of Catholic social teaching is what it calls a preferential option for the poor. In the *Compendium* this is treated along with the universal destination of goods and is dealt with relatively briefly, but one ought not to conclude from this that it is anything less than central in a Christian vision of the work of justice; and indeed the *Compendium* says that it is to be 'reaffirmed in all its force'. What it means is that, following the example of Jesus, a special attention must be given to the needs of all in our societies who are comprehended by the term 'marginalised'. The *Compendium* elucidates:

> This is an option, or a *special form* of primacy in the exercise of Christian charity, to which the whole tradition of the Church bears witness. It affects the life of each Christian inasmuch as he or she seeks to imitate the life of Christ, but it applies equally to our *social responsibilities* and hence to our manner of living, and to the logical decisions to be made concerning the ownership and use of goods. (182 [385]; emphasis in original)

As is usual the *Compendium* makes it clear that the Church's mission is not to establish a particular political or economic order, nor does it envisage only material deprivation. And as regards material poverty and deprivation:

> Christian realism, while appreciating on the one hand the praiseworthy efforts being made to defeat poverty, is cautious on the other hand regarding ideological positions and messianistic beliefs that sustain the illusion that it is possible to eliminate the problem of poverty completely from this world. (183)

Yet the duty to come to the aid of the poor is urgent and grave, and 'Our Lord warns us that we shall be separated from him if we fail to meet the serious needs of the poor and the little ones who are his brethren'. Quoting the Scripture and St Gregory the Great as well as the *Catechism* and the Second Vatican Council, the *Compendium* insists on the inextricability of the love commandment and the demands of justice.

> When we attend to the needs of those in want, we give them what is theirs, not ours. More than performing works of mercy, we are paying a debt of justice … [and] what is already due in justice is not to be offered as a gift of charity. (184[392/393])

Nor is the practice of charity limited to the giving of alms; rather it 'implies addressing the social and political dimensions of the problem of poverty'.

What we have in Catholic social teaching then is both a vision of the human and a corpus of principles whose intent is to promote that vision and translate it into practice. A reader whose first encounter with it is in these pages may already have been struck by the fact that it has been set out here in almost wholly secular terms. And indeed it is a feature of the teaching that it can be so expressed, and a feature of mainline Christian theology, which sees rational reflection on the experience of being human as a valid approach to the discovery of moral truth. An obvious advantage is that Catholic social teaching offers the makings of a language with which Christians can dialogue with those who do not share a Christian world view. Thus it was that Pope John XXIII was confident that the message of *Pacem in terris* could be understood and supported by people of good will outside of the Catholic Church. A disadvantage may be that it could lose touch with theological and especially biblical foundations that give it an enlivening distinctiveness and that can be a powerful source of motivation.

A point sometimes made also is that it is misleading to think of universally held and rationally agreed ideas of what is 'human'. Consider the differences between western feminist understandings of women's rights and some whose origin is in a middle eastern culture. Nor need we suppose that people of good will everywhere agree upon the *content* of individual rights: one has only to reflect on the differences there are about the content of the right to life. In these matters it is well to bear in mind that facile assumptions about commonalities can be as damaging to mutual understanding as can differences. But this can be overstated, and is perhaps overstated in some recent writing. It is not a small achievement that so many of the world's peoples can subscribe to the two great covenants on human rights, as well as numerous conventions and treaties, whose intent is to realise the aspirations of the UN Declaration of 1948. Differences notwithstanding, there is much in common between peoples as regards what is human and what makes for human flourishing. The postwar history of Europe offers hope, as does, for all its imperfections, the story of the European Union.

Meanwhile a commitment to human rights and to all that can help humanise our world is at the heart of the Church's mission to preach and bear witness to the Gospel of Jesus Christ. The social teaching makes it plain that the work of justice is not an optional but a central Gospel imperative. Some readers of the *Compendium* will be disappointed that it doesn't include the memorable dictum of the 1971 Synod's Work of Justice: that action on behalf of justice is a constitutive dimension preaching the Gospel. But what the *Compendium* does say may be read as a gloss on the Synod's message. For the *Compendium* affirms that the Church's social doctrine is both '*an integral part of her evangelising ministry*' and '*itself a valid instrument of evangelisation*' (emphasis in original). And, speaking of the 'profound links' that exist between 'evangelisation and human promotion' it recalls the words of Pope Paul VI:

> These include links of an anthropological order, because the one who is to be evangelised is not an abstract being but is subject to social and economic questions. They also include links in the theological order, since one cannot dissociate the plan of creation from the plan of Redemption. The latter plan touches the very concrete situations of injustice to be combated and of justice to be restored. They include links of the eminently evangelical order, which is that of charity: how in fact can one proclaim the new commandment without promoting in

> justice and in peace the true, authentic advancement of man?(66[86])

And so we may return to Pope Benedict's *Deus caritas est*, where in almost identical terms the connection between justice and agape is made. It is mistaken to suggest that this Pope's concern for social justice is any the less urgent than that of his predecessors, as may be seen from a reading of the second part of the encyclical. For him as for them it is not the business of the Church in the sense of Church as institution to seek to do the work of politics, though he makes it equally clear that this is a vocation of the lay faithful.

But, it is clear from the encyclical, even as regards the Church as institution, including the Church's magisterium:

> She cannot and must not remain on the sidelines in the fight for justice. She has to play her part through rational argument and she has to reawaken the spiritual energy without which justice, which always demands sacrifice, cannot prevail and prosper. A just society must be the achievement of politics, not of the Church. Yet the promotion of justice through efforts to bring about openness of mind and will to the demands of the common good is something which concerns the Church deeply. (28)

How deeply has already been hinted. For, though for Benedict social justice will never be so completely achieved as to make the work of 'social charity' redundant, men and women who follow the Gospel are called to shape a just society. And that, we must say, is part of what is meant by *ekklesia*, for, in the words of the encyclical:

> The Church's deepest nature is expressed in her three-fold responsibility: proclaiming the word of God (kerygma-martyria), celebrating the sacraments (leitourgia), and exercising the ministry of charity

(diakonia). These duties presuppose each other and are inseparable. For the Church, charity is not a kind of welfare activity which could equally well be left to others, but is a part of her nature, an indispensable expression of her very being. (25)

Notes

1 The phrase is from the *Constitution on the Church in the Modern World of Vatican II*. In the interests of easier reading I have kept references to a minimum and have all but avoided footnotes. But students of the *Compendium of the Social Doctrine of the Church* will find invaluable help in four works which are readily accessible: P. Corkery, *Companion to the Compendium*, Veritas, 2007; K. Himes et al. (eds) *Modern Catholic Social Teaching: Commentaries and Interpretations*, Georgetown University Press, 2005; J.A. Dwyer (ed.) *The New Dictionary of Catholic Social Thought*, Liturgical Press, 1994; D. Dorr, *Option for the Poor: A Hundred Years of Catholic Social Teaching*, Orbis Books, 2001.

2 The *Compendium* is a collection of official Church documents of various levels of authority, so what it contains is magisterial teaching. The term 'Catholic social thought' is of course a wider one, and the works cited in the previous footnote both exemplify and provide references to this. The insistence of some writers on a distinction between 'doctrine' and 'teaching' seems fussy, even when what is at stake is the important distinction between unchanging principle and contextual practical application. It is clear from the *Compendium* that Catholic social teaching at every level contains both immutable principle and what the US bishops have termed 'prudential judgement' as to concrete application. The misunderstanding whereby social teaching is thought not to bind conscience may be due in part to the fact that definitive claims are not made for norms of the order of prudential judgements.

3

CATHOLIC SOCIAL TEACHING: A Global Ethic

Eoin G. Cassidy

> It [the *Compendium*] is a sign of hope in the fact that religions and cultures today show openness to dialogue and sense the urgent need to join forces in promoting justice, fraternity, peace and the growth of the human person. (12)

One of the most striking aspects of the recently published *Compendium of the Social Doctrine of the Church* is the manner in which it avoids the temptation to restrict itself to addressing the Catholic Church but rather seeks to reach out to 'the people of our time, her travelling companions' – the universal family (3). Conscious of the urgency of the challenge to promote a global ethic the document proposes the core principles of the social teaching of the Catholic Church as 'the starting point for the promotion of an integral and solidary humanism' (7).

The authors of the *Compendium* see Catholic social teaching as making a contribution to the collective journey of humankind to the creation of 'a society reconciled in justice and love' (81). Each stage in that journey throws up its own particular challenges, ones shaped by the particular cultural configuration of the moment. Consequently, to assess the value of the *Compendium* for today, as distinct from its value as an historical record of Catholic social teaching, one needs to assess it in the context of an appreciation of the dominant cultural themes in today's world. By drawing upon an analysis of the legacy of modernity on the ethical landscape of the western world, this article will explore this issue.

Specifically, the article will examine the manner in which Catholic social teaching meets the challenges associated with the emergence of a relativist ethos in contemporary Liberalism. The question will be asked as to what extent and on what basis Catholic social teaching offers the possibility of challenging a cultural given that has the potential to undermine any belief in an objective truth over and against which the moral progress of individuals or society can be evaluated. Second, the article will examine the manner in which the principles of Catholic social teaching meet the challenges of an increasingly globalised world in which the goals of instrumental reason or the values of the market are seen by many to provide the template upon which behaviour either at an individual or a societal level is evaluated. To what extent can Catholic social teaching be called upon to challenge accepted 'capitalist' wisdom which places its trust in market forces often at the expense of values associated with the idea of solidarity or even of the concept of a just wage? Finally, the article will examine the manner in which Catholic social teaching has the ability to communicate its social gospel in the face of the growth in 'western' societies of an individualist anthropology that, at the extremes, has the potential to enclose itself within the narrow confines of a self-interest that rejects any ties of responsibility to the larger community.

In the service of the truth

'Modernity' increasingly appears as an umbrella concept for a spectrum of cultural developments that took place in Europe from the early part of the seventeenth century up until the middle of the twentieth century. Amongst the themes that have shaped Modernity has been the increasing acceptance of an individualist anthropology, the rise of instrumental reasoning and the development of a liberal culture that has flowed from an acceptance of the normative status of liberal democracy.

Liberalism emerged on the coat tails of the Reformation, a point in European history that marked the break-up of western Christendom and with that break-up the loss of a shared understanding of the values, beliefs and practices that define human existence. Over the last two hundred years liberal democracies have been developed as a political system that can accommodate pluralism. Today, the distinguishing feature of a liberal culture continues to be a tolerance of many divergent and in some cases incompatible world views. From such a perspective, pluralism is a fact of life, and one cannot but admire the success of liberal democracy in promoting the ideals of a tolerant and inclusive society. Nevertheless, there are those who would argue that it has also led to a cultural acceptance of a relativist ethos that has little sympathy for either the importance of tradition or the belief in the objectivity of moral values.

Published over twenty-five years ago, *After Virtue: A Study in Moral Theology*[1] gives expression to the celebrated philosopher Alasdair MacIntyre's view that the 'western' liberal culture is living in an age that has lost connection to the idea of Virtue – the idea that human life has a purpose and that the virtues are the pathways to that goal. We possess the words such as goodness, virtue, a virtuous life, etc. but we have lost our comprehension of a shared societal commitment to the concept of truth as central to human well-being – the recognition of an objective horizon of meaning and value that is the prerequisite, both theoretical and practical, of morality. In MacIntyre's opinion, in the absence of both a shared recognition that there is a goal constituted by the idea of the good that ought to be pursued for its own sake, and the sense of what might constitute this good, there is no rational way to gain moral agreement: hence, for all practical purposes, we are living in what he calls 'an emotivist culture'. As MacIntyre describes it:

> For what emotivism asserts is in central part that there are and can be no valid rational justification for any claims that objective and impersonal moral standards exist and hence that there are no such standards.[2]

In this deeply pessimistic appraisal of the state of contemporary culture, MacIntyre proclaims that emotivism has become embodied in our culture, and what was once morality has to some large degree disappeared, to be replaced by a theory which 'proclaims that all judgements are nothing but expressions of preference, attitude, feeling'.[3] Operating under the logic of instrumental reasoning where others are always means, never ends: the object of the exercise is to align other peoples's attitudes, feelings and preferences with one's own. It is MacIntyre's firm conviction that the increasing predominance of emotivism in contemporary 'western' culture represents a grave cultural loss.[4] It is a viewpoint that has not changed over the course of the intervening years. Furthermore, if he is correct, the contemporary liberal culture cannot sustain the wherewithal to create a moral community. In the absence of a belief that there is a purpose to human existence as well as some level of agreement as to what that purpose might entail, Liberalism neither provides a basis for moral discourse nor a context for rationally securing agreement on any moral issue.

While MacIntyre's commitment to the concept of truth as central to human well-being and the importance which he attaches to this issue is a stance that places him in opposition to the relativist ethos of Liberalism, it is nevertheless one that strikes a sympathetic chord with core Catholic social teaching. There can be no more potent symbolic expression of the importance of this fact than that provided by the final homily delivered by the then Cardinal Ratzinger on the steps of St Peter's on 19 April 2005, the day before the conclave at which he was elected Pope Benedict XVI:

> Relativism, which is letting oneself be tossed and swept along by every wind of teaching, looks like the only

> attitude acceptable to today's standards ... We are moving toward a dictatorship of relativism which does not recognise anything as definitive and has as its highest value one's own ego and one's own desires.

Among the truths to which we aspire, truth about the human good is of particular importance, and the Catholic Church's opposition to the viewpoint that moral principles have no objective standards is something that finds a clear resonance in the *Compendium*. The seriousness of this issue for the authors of the *Compendium* can be adduced from the introduction to the *Compendium* which finds its focus in a section entitled 'At the service of the full truth about man' (13 and following) and it is reflected in this passage: 'The deepest meaning of human existence, in fact, is revealed in the free quest for that truth capable of giving direction and fullness to life.' (15)

Human existence is shaped by the search for meaning and value. Not only is the question of the existence and accessibility of truth a defining issue in terms of this quest, it is also one that takes on a particular urgency in the face of the unique challenge posed by the relativist ethos of today's world. That the authors of the *Compendium* were in no doubt about the significance of this challenge can be seen in the following passage from the introduction: 'The first of the great challenges facing humanity today is that of *the truth itself of the being who is man*.' (16; emphasis in original)

As one reads this section, it becomes clear that Catholic social teaching testifies to the belief that the universal search for meaning is not one that is undertaken in vain. Furthermore, the *Compendium* squarely situates the significance of Catholic social teaching in the context of that which provides precious insights into 'the truth about man's place in nature and in human society' (14). Ultimately, the importance attached to the issue of truth in the *Compendium* can only be grasped to the extent that one understands the Catholic Church's sense of mission as 'in the service of the truth'. For Catholic social teaching, this is a stance that accepts the normative character of the historical revelation of truth in the person of Christ. Against those who would argue that this in effect replaces the moral relativism of contemporary culture with a form of moral fundamentalism, it must be recognised that Catholic social teaching not only gives voice to a commitment to truth but also to the transcendence of truth, a stance that eschews the extremes of both moral fundamentalism and of moral relativism. As it says:

> [It] is important for the world to recognise the Church as a reality of history and a leaven in history, so too, is it important for the Church to recognise what she has received from history and from the development of the human race. (18)

As the quotation makes clear, the authors of the *Compendium* wish to give expression to the not-yet or transcendent character of revelation that does justice to the historical character of human existence. This they achieve by correctly situating Catholic social teaching in the context of that God-given journey towards truth that, in every generation and in every culture, gives meaning to individuals and society alike.

Human rights and human nature

The issue of globalisation is one of only three key cultural challenges facing humanity that are identified by the authors of the *Compendium*. As they put it:

> The third challenge is *globalisation*, the significance of which is much wider and more profound than simple economic globalisation, since history has witnessed the opening of a new era that concerns humanity's destiny. (16)

From their point of view, the challenge facing society today is to create the conditions that will make possible the reality of a universal community. To meet this challenge, 'solidarity too must become globalised' (321).

Commentators on today's global culture like to highlight the emergence of a more free-floating individualist anthropology. Removed from any sense of belonging to a tradition and no longer bound by ties to any particular community, the individual is paradoxically both a citizen of the world and yet no citizen at all. Whatever the truth of these observations, it is undoubtedly the case that the recent economic and technological revolutions in themselves alone would never have given rise to the cultural phenomenon of globalisation. The challenge over recent decades has been therefore to construct an ethic for a globalised world that both acknowledges the cultural reality of an individualist anthropology and yet strives to create the conditions that will promote the idea of a universal community. One of the ways in which society, over the past fifty years, has attempted to meet this challenge is in and through the construction of a range of human rights covenants that purport to have a universal applicability. In a remarkable acknowledgement of the nobility of this effort the late Pope John Paul II stated that the adoption of the Universal Declaration of Human Rights in 1948 could be seen as 'a true milestone on the path of humanity's moral progress' (152). In agreement with this perspective the authors of the *Compendium* acknowledge that: 'An adequate solidarity in the era of globalisation requires that human rights be defended.' (365)

The authors of the *Compendium* are of the conviction that it is only a commitment to human rights that will give society the resources to promote the idea of a global community in which all see themselves as members of the human family with both rights and responsibilities that flow from that reality. However, translating the idea of a global community into reality is crucially dependent on the belief that it is possible to transcend the culturally conditioned character of social discourse and to discern core societal values/rights that are culturally invariant. This is no easy task. For instance, it could be argued that many of the current internationally recognised human rights provisions are driven by concerns that have their focus in the specifics of 'western' culture – an emphasis on a particular way of understanding the ideals of freedom and equality that have their origins in the legacy of the European Enlightenment and do not translate all that easily into value systems of those from very different cultures. Furthermore, the very suggestion that these 'western' ideals have universal applicability is one that carries with it more than a hint of cultural imperialism. For example, in many African, Middle Eastern and Oriental countries the ideal of individual freedom is valued but clearly subordinated to a prior set of relationships that encompasses both the extended family as well as the larger society. Similarly, in many of these countries, the idea of equality, while valued, is nevertheless subordinated to the exercise of a hierarchical set of relationships based on age and gender that determine the appropriate exercise of authority.

A belief in the culturally invariant character of human rights provisions can also be challenged from the perspective of increasingly rapid generational change within what is loosely called 'western' culture. One only has to think of the manner in which the feminist critique of the woman as wife, mother and homemaker has in the past twenty years reshaped core human rights provisions on marriage, the family and the place of women in the workplace.[5] Or indeed, the manner in which the emergence of a more secular western culture contributes to the emergence of newly formulated so-called rights that call for a re-definition of commonly accepted existing rights. One thinks for example of the manner in which the newly formulated so-called rights such as the 'right to choose' and the 'right to die with dignity' challenge the primacy of the 'right to life' and/or the manner in which this right was traditionally understood, and indeed raise critical questions as to what, if any, qualifications can and must be placed upon the exercise of this right.[6]

As those who charted the course of the 1948 UN Universal Declaration perceptively observed, everything is based upon the concept of human dignity – 'the recognition of the inherent dignity and of the equal and inalienable rights of all members of the human family' (Preamble, 1948 UN Universal Declaration). The challenge is to chart the parameters of human dignity – to uncover what rights flow from the concept of human dignity and how one would sustain one's choice of rights in the face of competing views. Those who framed the 1948 UN Universal Declaration did not imagine that they had discovered the whole truth about human beings and human rights and yet they did not flinch from the task of setting out a list of what they regarded as universal, indivisible and inalienable rights.[7] In the aftermath of the holocaust they were only too aware that the Universal Declaration could not be held hostage to fortune awaiting definitive agreement on a universally accepted theory of human nature.

However, despite the widespread acceptance of the human rights provisions outlined in the Universal Declaration the issue of the truth about human nature cannot be avoided. The contemporary cultural milieu is very different to that faced by those who framed the 1948 UN Universal Declaration. In the light of increasing awareness of the cultural conditioned character of so many of the human rights provisions and the liberal and secular ethos of today's world that rejects the idea of an objective and/or transcendent source of meaning, the question must be asked as to what extent, if at all, we can legitimately speak of rights as inalienable. This issue cannot be avoided in that both the idea and the reality of a global community are ultimately dependent on the shared belief that there are some set of values that can be deemed to be both universal and inalienable because they flow from the inherent dignity of the human person. The challenge is then to distinguish that which *is* from that which *is not* culturally invariant and to outline the basis upon which that distinction is made. Some of the differences are merely of a semantic nature; others, however, have their roots in very different views of human nature. To put it concretely, to what extent can one condemn aspects of the Islamic Sharia law[8] or for that matter, to what extent can one condemn the US practice of rendition or those surrounding the existence of the detention centre at Guantanamo Bay as violations of human rights?[9]

Based on the belief in the social character of human nature and the objectivity of values, the origin of which is to be found in the creative will of God, Catholic social teaching has a unique contribution to make to those who seek to challenge the cultural bias of a liberal and secular ethos. It offers strong support to those who stress the dangers of regarding human rights as in some way free floating – independent of some concept of the inherent nature of the dignity of human nature. Even more importantly, it teaches with conviction that the vision of a human nature that in turn gives rise to the concept of human rights is one that is discernible in and through attention to the natural law.

> The exercise of freedom implies a reference to a natural moral law, of a universal character, that precedes and unites all rights and duties. The natural law is nothing other than the light of intellect infused within us by God. Thanks to this, we know what must be done and what must be avoided. (140)

As the authors of the *Compendium* also make clear, Catholic social teaching provides for a vision of human rights that is both grounded in and flows from a vision of the person in his/her relationship with God.

> The ultimate source of human rights is not found in the mere will of human beings, in the reality of the State, in public powers, but in man himself and in God his Creator. These rights are universal, inviolable and inalienable. (153)

One of the oft repeated criticisms of the contemporary emphasis on a human rights ethics is that it could be interpreted as offering support to an over-individualist vision of human nature.[10] In this respect, Catholic social teaching, which seeks to balance rights with duties, provides a valuable corrective. As the *Compendium* states:

> This bond [between rights and duties] also has a social dimension: 'in human society to one man's right there corresponds a duty in all other persons: the duty namely, of acknowledging and respecting the right in question'. (156)

In laying stress on the social character of humankind the authors of the *Compendium* introduce the idea of the common good and the responsibility of everyone to promote the common good, the demands of which are 'strictly connected to respect for and the integral promotion of the person and his fundamental rights' (166).

The common good and the sum of individual preferences

One of the core concepts of Catholic social teaching, the concept of the common good, is perceived by the authors of the *Compendium* as indicating 'the sum total of social conditions which allow people, either as groups or as individuals, to reach their fulfilment more fully and more easily' (164). It is the social and community dimension of the moral good and the authentic reason for the very existence of the diverse forms of social organisation (165). Clearly, this concept is of the first importance in the context of meeting the challenges of today's culture – to uphold the ideal of an ethical society or a global ethic as distinct from one shaped solely by the exigencies of the market.

Earlier, reference was made to Alasdair MacIntyre's critique of the individualist character of today's liberal culture. As he perceptively observes, a liberal culture not only occludes any shared concept of the common good but even lacks space for the idea of the common good. In a cultural milieu that refuses to accept the objectivity of moral values any debate that seeks to achieve some consensus surrounding the common good is ultimately sterile. In point of fact, in such a cultural milieu, the ethical concept of the common good can never be perceived as anything more than the sum of individual preferences – an idea that has very little if anything in common with the concept of the good life.

From the standpoint of economic theory, the emergence of an individualist culture is often associated with the rise of Capitalism. More recently, it is perceived as one of the factors that has contributed to the emergence of a globalised world replete with multi-national global corporations. This individualist ethos has a strong instrumentalist focus, one which poses a different but equally challenging point of reference to those who would seek to uphold the ethical character of the concept of the common good. The basic premise of ethical ideals such as human rights and the concept of the common good is the view that human beings are subjects – ends in themselves and ought never to be treated as objects – as means to an end. The instrumentalist ethos of the global market is one that promotes the ideal of efficiency to the virtual exclusion of all other values. Unfortunately, this has the effect of inverting or subverting the ends/means distinction that is the bedrock of any coherent concept of the common good.

The individualist and instrumentalist ethos of contemporary society whose contours are shaped by the exigencies of the market and the world of the market place is one that can have little sympathy with ideals associated with the work of community building. Neither is it one that can easily espouse the idea of social solidarity or even the idea of the common good except insofar as it is defined as the sum of individual preferences. By over-identifying the development of a globalised world with economic progress in a manner that loses sight of any real distinction between ethics and economics, western society is in danger of subordinating concerns with creating a global community to the exigencies of the market.

One of the most trenchant critiques of the individualist ethos of a capitalist culture is to be seen in the work of the celebrated American sociologist Robert Bellah, which explores the significance of individualism on the American psyche. In the course of his study he offers the following historical example that shows the importance of maintaining a clear distinction between the concept of the common good and the sum of individual preferences. The example is taken from the Douglas/Lincoln debate of 1858 which he regards as a defining moment in American history. The issue was whether slavery should be extended to the territories in the West. As Bellah recounts it:

> Douglas took the line of popular sovereignty: if they want slavery, let them have slavery. The basis of Douglas's position was a utilitarian liberalism that asked only for the summing of preferences, not about the moral quality of the preferences. But Lincoln said that slavery was wrong, that it contradicted the nation's most fundamental principles and should not be extended to the territories no matter what the majority there might want ... Lincoln's position drew upon biblical and republican sources and committed not only to the notion of an objective moral order but also to the notion that individuals live in a society that has a common good beyond the sum of individual goods.[11]

In a further comment upon the significance of this distinction Bellah continues:

> If we apply Lincoln's words to our situation we can say that the house today is divided not by slavery but by deepening class divisions. Douglas had no problem with a house divided, since he saw society as nothing more than the sum of individual choices and their consequences. Lincoln, however, judged certain conditions to be objectively wrong and held society accountable for changing them.[12]

As the title suggests, Catholic social teaching is founded upon a vision of human nature that both acknowledges the social and community dimension to human flourishing and gives due recognition to the ethical consequences which flow from that vision. Furthermore, it is precisely the desire to stress the social character of human life that gives rise to the emphasis that the authors of the *Compendium* place on the concept of the common good as 'nothing less than the social and community dimension of the moral good' (164). In laying emphasis on the ethical character of the concept of the common good Catholic social teaching is drawing attention to the classical distinction between intrinsic and extrinsic goods in a manner that distances itself from the utilitarian reasoning characteristic of a liberal culture. In this context, it is not surprising that Catholic social teaching on the common good is marked by an emphatic rejection of the opinions of those who perceive society to be nothing more than the sum of individual choices and their consequences.[13]

Catholic social teaching on the common good is founded on the belief that the family, the state, etc. – each expression of social life – exists for a purpose and that this goal or common good is, as the *Compendium* states, 'the authentic reason for its very existence' (165). Furthermore, it is this vision that allows one to see the ethical implications of the social character of human living – the fact that the human person exists with others and for others – which requires each person to seek for the common good that is to be found in each of the various forms of social life into which he/she is inserted. Finally, Catholic social teaching on the common good has the potential to offer a much needed corrective to over-individualist and relativist character of today's liberal culture where ethical considerations at societal level risk being interpreted in terms of individual preferences.[14]

The emerging phenomenon of globalisation is one whose values are increasingly set by the exigencies of the market. In that respect it is an individualist culture that espouses a pragmatic set of values that places the goal of efficiency over all others, and where ethics is valued to the extent that it promotes this goal. Culture shaped by the principles of the 'market' is not one that finds it easy to address the ethical concept of fairness, whether it is a fair wage or even the idea of fair trade. At the extremes, the economic forces at play in a global economy are those that encourage what has rather tellingly been described as a race to the bottom. By contrast, Catholic social teaching is based on a vision of the inalienable dignity of each individual as loved by Christ where human beings are understood as subjects and never as objects. In such a perspective, issues of fairness, from whatever quarter, can never be ignored or subordinated to the exigencies of the market. Furthermore, by acknowledging the importance of the requirement of solidarity Catholic social teaching not only gives recognition to the ideal of a universal community but seeks ways of shaping the phenomenon of globalisation in this direction.

In today's culture, which shows evidence of an over-reliance on the values associated with an individualist anthropology, there has never been more need for the tradition of Catholic social teaching on the social character of human nature. The same can be said for a culture such as ours that is increasingly shaped by an over-reliance on instrumental reasoning where everything and everybody is judged in terms of their present effectiveness and their future prospects. In such a cultural milieu, not only is there little place for charters of fundamental rights but ultimately all values are marginalised in favour of more short-term utilitarian concerns.

To conclude, a culture animated by the principles of Catholic social teaching as outlined in the *Compendium* has a unique contribution to make to the humanisation of contemporary culture. It has the potential to bring hope to a global world marked by the rootlessness of an individualist culture. By challenging the belief that people are subject to the market with the conviction that the market should be at the service of human beings, Catholic social teaching has also the capability to create solidarity among peoples and to bring justice to a world too often marked by the economic and social divisions. The lessons of history remind us however that this contribution will only be made if the core principles of Catholic social teaching are inculturated in a manner that meets the emerging concerns of each new generation.

Notes

1 Duckworth Press, London, 1981.
2 Ibid., p. 19.
3 Ibid., p. 14.
4 Ibid., p. 22.
5 In sections 294 and 295 the *Compendium* offers a valuable reflection on women and the right to work that seeks to situate the exercise of this right in the context of a rejection of a strictly private conception of the family or a strictly economic view of work. In the course of this analysis, they highlight the urgent need to overcome obstacles in the path of the exercise of women's rights in the workplace. A more detailed treatment of these issues a) under the rubric of the right to equal treatment between men and women is to be found in sections 144–7, and b) under the rubric of the relationship between family and work is to be found in sections 248–51.
6 This recent cultural development runs counter to a core premise of Catholic social teaching that sees in the development of human rights 'one of the most significant attempts to respond effectively to the inescapable demands of human dignity' (153). In section 155 the authors of the *Compendium* make reference to the list of rights drawn up by the late Pope John Paul II in the encyclical Centesimus annus. As they say: 'The first right presented in this list is the right to life, from conception to its natural end, which is the condition for the exercise of all other rights and, in particular, implies the illicitness of every form of procured abortion and of euthanasia.'
7 In the course of an excellent commentary on the process that led to the 1948 UN Declaration of Human Rights, Ann Glendon observes: 'But they harboured no illusions about how deep the

agreement they had discovered went. Maritain [the eminent French philosopher] liked to tell the story of how a visitor at one meeting expressed astonishment that champions of violently opposed ideologies had been able to agree on a list of fundamental rights. The man was told: "Yes, we agree about the rights but on condition no one asks us why".' *A World Made New: Eleanor Roosevelt and the Universal Declaration of Human Rights*, New York, Random House Trade Paperbacks, 2001, p. 77.

8 Although the *Compendium* makes no explicit reference to Sharia law, nevertheless the inappropriateness of the refusal to acknowledge the legitimacy of the civic space can be seen in the following passage: 'In fact, the political community and the Church are autonomous and independent of each other in their own fields ... Indeed, it can be affirmed that the distinction between religion and politics and the principle of religious freedom constitute a specific achievement of Christianity and one of its fundamental historical and cultural contributions.' (50)

9 See the following passage from the *Compendium*: '... there exists therefore, a right to defend oneself from terrorism. However, this right cannot be exercised in the absence of moral and legal norms, because the struggle against terrorists must be carried out with respect for human rights and for the principles of a State ruled by law.' (154)

10 See the following passage from the *Compendium*: '... an excessive affirmation of equality can give rise to an individualism in which each one claims his own rights without wishing to be answerable for the common good.' (158) For an unequivocal statement of the relational and social dimension of human nature, see section 110.

11 *Habits of the Heart*, Los Angeles, University of California Press, 1996, xxxiv–xxxv.

12 Ibid., p. 35.

13 See the following passage from the *Compendium*: 'The common good does not consist in the simple sum of the particular goods of each subject of a social entity.' (164)

14 See the following passage from the *Compendium*: 'Those responsible for government are required to interpret the common good of their country not only according to the

guidelines of the majority but also according to the effective good of all the members of the community, including the minority.' (169)

SECTION TWO

Faith and Politics

4

CHRIST AND CAESAR: Reflections on Faith and Politics in the *Compendium of the Social Doctrine of the Church*

John Murray

'What has Jerusalem to do with Athens?' This provocative rhetorical question was asked centuries ago, in the time of the early Church Fathers, by Tertullian.[1] The implied answer was: 'Nothing!' Tertullian's point was to express extreme doubt about whether Christianity (Jerusalem) ought to show any positive interest in secular philosophy (Athens). Christian faith was to remain pure, not defiled or distracted by any mere worldly wisdom. Today, perhaps a similar kind of question might be: 'What has the Holy See to do with Washington DC?' In this version of the ancient question, the Holy See stands for the Catholic faith and Washington DC stands for politics. Still at the global level, we could phrase the question, 'What has Roman Catholicism to do with the United Nations?' Taking a more European view, we might phrase the question 'What has the Vatican to do with Brussels?' At the national level in Ireland, the question could be: 'What has Archbishop's House to do with Leinster House?'[2] Those who take a Tertullian-like approach to the faith, wishing to preserve its 'purity', will probably answer this modern question, in any of these forms, with a similar answer to that given by Tertullian: 'Nothing! Faith has nothing to do with politics.' Catholic faith and secular politics are to be seen as completely separate. For many today, this is what the modern doctrine of 'separation of Church and State' means, and it is regarded as a doctrine that both the modern secular democratic state and the modern post-Vatican II Church ought to adhere to in every respect. Such people might be somewhat disturbed with the recent publication of the *Compendium of the Social Doctrine of the Church*, within whose pages one can find the Church expressing teachings on the rights of nations (157),[3] population control (234), the relationship between labour and capital (276–80), the role of the free market (347–50), institutions and democracy (408–9), the value of international organisations (440–3), the use of biotechnology (472–80), and many other seemingly 'political' subjects.

Others might be delighted with a publication dealing with such issues. For these people, or at least some of them, the answer to the questions mentioned above is: 'Everything! Faith has everything to do with politics.' Christian faith is not to be separated from secular politics at all. 'At last,' such readers might exclaim, 'the Church is speaking a language that all can identify with, a *relevant* language about topics that concern modern people.' For this kind of approach, political issues are at the heart of what it means to be a modern Christian or Catholic. Church and state are not completely separate; politics and faith are intimately related.

Does the *Compendium* support the second answer ('Everything!')? Or ought the Church keep to the seeming purity of Tertullian's approach ('Nothing!')? The few reflections here, though limited and claiming no great originality or comprehensiveness, offer some pointers to an answer to these questions, relying mainly on what the *Compendium* itself has to say on the matter, particularly in its introduction.

First, let it be immediately said that the two approaches above, as described here, are extremes; in fact, they are caricatures. This is deliberate. These extremes or caricatures are presented here to make a point. This point is that the Church's answer to the question of what faith has to do with politics avoids the extremes, holding the two approaches in a delicate balance, drawing from the strengths of each and eschewing their weaknesses. Nothing in these reflections is meant to claim that anyone or any group holds these extreme views in their pure form. Speaking about Nothing and Everything approaches is meant to indicate opposing tendencies that can be found in society and its various civil groupings, in the Church, and in individuals' hearts and minds. The Nothing (to do with politics) approach is a name for an extreme tendency to detachment from the temporal world and its concerns; the Everything (to do with politics) approach names the opposite tendency, that of attachment to the temporal world and its concerns. The approach defended and explained here, the Church's approach, is one that is somewhere in the middle of these two extremes of detachment and attachment.[4] This approach does not answer with an all or nothing answer; it does not reply 'Nothing' or 'Everything' to the questions posed in the opening paragraph above. To understand the approach put forward here, which is that found in the *Compendium*, it will be helpful to look at what the two extremes are in more detail and to try to understand their attraction. It is important to recognise that both extremes grasp some of the truth, although each is one-sided, narrow and incomplete and, therefore, a distorted view of the truth about the relationship between faith and politics.

The two extreme tendencies, Nothing and Everything, detachment and attachment, can also be given other names. These can be uncovered by asking what the ideal Christian is, or what the ideal Christian Church is. The detachment tendency answers: the ideal Christian is a monk, the ideal Church a monastery. The attachment tendency answers: the ideal Christian is a social activist, the ideal Church a justice and peace group or lobby.

Let's look at what these answers imply.[5] The detachment tendency or the exclusively monastic ideal or model of faith considers this world and its concerns to be relatively unimportant. Indeed, this world can be seen as a distraction or even temptation. What really matters is the next world, the world after death. The purpose of being alive is to get to heaven, to save one's soul. The essential things are whatever directly contributes to this purpose, things such as prayer, worship, faith in religious doctrines, sacramental practice, devotions, penitential fasting, pilgrimages, avoiding personal sins, and so on. The human person is the soul; one's body is not one's real self. This world is seen as a place of 'exile', a 'valley of tears',[6] a place of testing. If one passes the test, which has been set by God, one can get to heaven. Heaven is seen as a place where one's soul goes after death, perhaps once it has been purified in purgatory. Heaven consists in the beatific vision, in which one contemplates God in all his infinite glory, thus reaching personal happiness and 'eternal rest'.

This heavenly contemplation is not bodily; nor is it particularly communal as such. There seems to be no intrinsic link between life now in this world, in the body, and eternal life in heaven, in the soul. Life now, with all its temporal and bodily concerns, is seen as, at best, a necessary evil to be endured. Detachment from the temporal is seen as essential if one is not to be distracted from what is really important. People in the Church who are particularly detached from the temporal, people such as monks, priests and religious, are seen as the real Catholics and lay people are seen as second-class citizens, those who couldn't reach the ideal but who can hope to get to heaven with the help of those who are truly holy. This monastic ideal sees faith and politics as very different things, very separate areas.

The attachment tendency presents a complete contrast to the monastic ideal. We might name this opposite tendency the social activist ideal or model. This ideal considers the world and its concerns to be of the greatest importance. Heaven, and religion insofar as it is focused on heaven and eternal concerns, is seen as a distraction and even a temptation. What really matters is this world, the world before death. The purpose of being alive is to make this world a better place. The essential things are whatever directly contribute to this purpose, things such as social awareness, consciousness raising, social justice, community, campaigns on specific issues of the day, lobbying, concrete work for the poor, fasting to raise money for the needy, the option for the poor, and so on. The human person is the body, and perhaps the mind and emotions (but not the soul, as such). This world is seen as our home, a home in need of repair by our work. The purpose of life is to be happy now and to help others to be happy now too, especially by eliminating suffering and injustice: 'Let us build the city of God'.[7] Heaven is seen as this world transformed by justice, an ideal future on earth. God is seen as a lover of justice and an inspirer of social concern and action with, and for, the poor and oppressed. To act for justice is to win God's favour and to be truly human. Being 'holy' is not seen as particularly attractive. Attachment to this world and its concerns is seen as essential, and those in the Church who seem preoccupied with the next world, especially monks, priests and religious, are seen as misguided, unnecessary and out-of-date. This kind of Christian faith is seen as a 'Vatican II' kind of faith; the detachment approach, the monastic ideal, is seen as the pre-Vatican II model that the People of God have now discarded at last.

As said above, both extremes are caricatures, presented here to make a point. As is often the case with caricatures, each of them embodies some truth. It is true that we are called to be detached from worldly concerns to some extent and to have our attention set on heaven and spiritual matters. Several scripture passages can be called to mind suggesting this. Here are a few examples.

> Do not store up for yourselves treasures on earth, where moth and rust consume and where thieves break in and steal; but store up for yourselves treasures in heaven, where neither moth nor rust consumes and where thieves do not break in and steal. For where your treasure is, there your heart will be also. (Mt 6:20-21)

> But strive first for the Kingdom of God and his righteousness, and all these things will be given to you as well. (Mt 6:33)

> Jesus answered [Pilate], 'My kingdom is not from this world. If my kingdom were from this world, my followers would be fighting to keep me from being handed over to the Jews. But as it is, my kingdom is not from here'. (Jn 18:36)

> Where is the wise man? Where is the scribe? Where is the debater of this age? Has not God made foolish the wisdom of the world? For since, in the wisdom of God, the world did not know God through wisdom, it pleased God through the folly of what we preach to save those who believe. For Jews demand signs and Greeks seek wisdom, but we preach Christ crucified, a stumbling block to Jews and folly to Gentiles, but to those who are called, both Jews and Greeks, Christ the power of God and the wisdom of God. (1 Cor 1:20-24)

> Now we have received not the spirit of the world, but the Spirit which is from God, that we might understand the gifts bestowed on us by God. And we impart this in words not taught by human wisdom but taught by the Spirit, interpreting spiritual truths to those who possess the Spirit. (1 Cor 2:12-13)[8]

Passages such as these, and the example of Christ who refused to be the political Messiah that many Jews of his time expected and hoped for, along with other aspects of our Christian faith and practice (not least the historical emergence of monasticism) have led to the detachment tendency being seen by many as essential to the ideal type of Christian faith and life. It is undoubtedly true that prayer, worship, devotions, and so on, are centrally important in the Catholic tradition. However, the attachment tendency, the social activist ideal, can point in its turn to scripture and to tradition to back it up. The creation accounts of Genesis repeatedly emphasise that God saw his creation as 'good ... very good' (see Gen 1:10, 12, 18, 21, 25, 31). God created human beings 'in his image' (Gen 1:27). The

Incarnation itself suggests strongly that God views the human body as precious: 'the Word became flesh and lived among us' (Jn 1:14). Jesus did not only preach repentance and forgiveness of sins, he also healed the sick, fed the hungry and raised the dead. St Paul, whilst emphasising the importance of the spiritual dimension, did not despise the body: 'Do you not know that your body is a temple of the Holy Spirit within you, which you have from God? You are not your own; you were bought with a price. So glorify God in your body' (1 Cor 6:19-20). There are a host of biblical passages exhorting us to be socially concerned and to act for justice, especially justice for the poor – see, for example, Ex 23:6-9; Is 58:1-12; Amos 5:21-24; Mt 25:31-46; Lk 16:19-31; Rom 12-14; and many more.[9] Church history and tradition can be read as backing up the social activist model of being a Christian. It is a matter of historical fact that monasticism, for all its valuable witness to the eternal perspective in Christian life, has not been put forward as obligatory for all Christians. Indeed, social activism of various kinds, including that of monks and monasteries, has been part and parcel of Christian practice since the beginning of the Faith.[10]

So it would seem that both tendencies, detachment and attachment, the monastic ideal and the social activist ideal, have some truth to them, and can be backed up by scripture and tradition. Each is attractive in its own way and each has weaknesses whenever it rejects the other. It would seem plausible to suggest that the best thing would be to accept both tendencies/ideals and combine them into one more adequate ideal, one that recognises this world *and* the next, the temporal *and* the eternal, the body *and* the soul, prayer *and* charity, faith *and* morals, and so on, rather than focusing only on one dimension of Christian faith. This is a 'both/and' rather than an 'either/or' approach. It is the approach taken in the *Compendium of the Social Doctrine of the Church*.

The remainder of this chapter will look briefly at the *Compendium* and how it explains its rationale from a Christian faith perspective. The focus here is mainly on the introductory paragraphs of the *Compendium*. A more comprehensive treatment of this issue would look at the document in full, as a faith perspective permeates the whole document. In particular, one would need to examine the specifically biblical sections that preface each of the main parts in Part Two of the *Compendium* – parts dealing with the family,[11] human work, economic life, the political community, the international community, safeguarding the environment and the promotion of peace. There is a detailed index of references at the end of the document, listing the Bible and Church document passages cited in the *Compendium*. Even a quick glance at this index gives one a clear impression of how thoroughly the Bible and documents of faith from the tradition are integrated throughout the *Compendium*.

Our interest here, however, is in the opening paragraphs of the *Compendium*, where it examines directly the relationship between Christian faith and politics.[12] (Hopefully readers will not skip these introductory paragraphs, and indeed the first few chapters, in their haste to see what the Church has to say on specific issues. These first few chapters lay the theological foundation for what follows.) The introduction is entitled 'An Integral and Solidary Humanism'. This title gives us a clear indication of the approach of the *Compendium* to the relationship between faith and politics. First, the social doctrine of the Church is concerned with developing 'humanism'. There is a clear and central focus on the human person. Second, this humanism is 'integral'. This word 'integral' is not a very commonly used term, but it is essential to understand it if one is to appreciate what the *Compendium* is about. It is one of the most important words in the whole document. 'Integral' means *complete* or *whole*. Third, the humanism that the Church promotes is 'solidary'. This is an even more uncommon term than 'integral'.[13] 'Solidary' means *having a community of interests and responsibilities*. So we could rephrase the opening title as 'A Complete and Communal Humanism'. This is what Catholic social doctrine is all about. We look in more detail at these ideas in the following paragraphs.

Humanism is concerned with the good of the human person and his or her concerns and needs. An *integral* humanism is one that is not partial or incomplete. Integral humanism deals with the human person in all his or her (and, in 'solidary humanism', *their*) integrated complexity: body and soul, material and spiritual, individual and social. In the very first paragraph of the *Compendium* we find the following:

> Salvation, which the Lord Jesus obtained 'at a price' (1 Cor 6:20; cf. 1 Pet 1:18-19), is achieved in the new life that awaits the righteous after death, but it also permeates this world in the realities of the economy and labour, of technology and communications, of society and politics, of the international community and the relations among cultures and peoples. 'Jesus came to bring integral salvation, one which embraces the whole person and all mankind, and opens up the wondrous prospect of divine filiation.'[14]

In keeping with the general style of the document, and of many Church documents, these two sentences are dense and rich in meaning. It takes effort and patience to read and 'unpack' such sentences. The humanism of the *Compendium* is one focused on Jesus, 'the one Saviour and goal of history'.[15] We are not talking here of any kind of secular humanism, focused on only this life, on temporal concerns alone. It is a thoroughly religious humanism, one that does not hesitate to speak right from the start of 'salvation'. The salvation spoken of is found only through Christ. It is a salvation for all people, and so the Church speaks to all. However, it is not a narrowly focused salvation, saving only our souls, saving us only after death: it is *integral* salvation. It includes both this worldly and otherworldly perspectives and it treats these as intrinsically related; it echoes elements of the two tendencies looked at above, both detachment and attachment. Integral salvation includes both my body and my soul; and it embraces both me as an individual and me as a member of a social body, a community centred in the Church but extending as far as the bounds of the human race itself. This salvation is not confined to this life, but is 'achieved in the new life that awaits the righteous after death' and 'opens up the wondrous prospect of divine filiation' (in other words, we share in God's own life as his 'sons' by our union with the Son – see Rom 8:14-17). Nevertheless, this salvation already 'permeates this world' with all its political aspects – which the first paragraph of the *Compendium* lists in specific detail.

From its very beginning then, the *Compendium* speaks a pilgrim language of Christian faith with confidence that such faith can be inclusive of all that is good in human life and inclusive of all who are the Church's 'travelling companions' (2). Two central concepts related to Christian humanism in this pilgrim language are 'dignity' and 'vocation' – as seen in paragraph 3:

> In fact, when the Church 'fulfils her mission of proclaiming the Gospel, she bears witness to man, in the name of Christ, to his dignity and his vocation to the communion of persons. She teaches him the demands of justice and peace in conformity with divine wisdom.' *This doctrine has its own profound unity, which flows from Faith in a whole and complete salvation, from Hope in a fullness of justice, and from Love which makes all mankind truly brothers and sisters in Christ*: it is the expression of God's love for the world, which he so loved 'that he gave his only Son' (Jn 3:16).[16]

The Gospel proclaims that man has dignity and a vocation to community. The Church is bound in Christ to 'bear witness to man', a phrase that includes both witnessing to Christ and witnessing to the human person *at the same time*.[17] We see an emphasis in paragraph 3 of the *Compendium* on 'a whole and complete salvation ... fullness of justice ... all mankind', phrases that echo the central concept of 'integral and solidary humanism'. Christian faith eschews narrowness and seeks a holistic vision of man – in the light of Christ, who was and is God-made-Man, divine Word made human flesh.

Paragraph 4 of the *Compendium* develops the idea of human dignity by linking it with the ideas of transcendence and God's love. 'Discovering that they are loved by God, people come to understand their own transcendent dignity, they learn not to be satisfied with only themselves but to encounter their neighbour in a network of relationships that are ever more authentically human.' Human dignity is not independent of God: it is grounded in God and in his love for all mankind. Coming to know more and more deeply the truth of faith that 'God is love',[18] people are empowered to understand themselves more deeply. Knowledge of God and knowledge of man are intimately linked. The monk who seeks to know God and his holiness, and the social activist who seeks to know the human person and his needs, to refer back to the two tendencies outlined in my opening pages, are not necessarily or rightly understood as separate; in fact, each can flourish only by including the other. One does not come to know God by ignoring man, nor man by ignoring God (cf. 1 Jn 2:3-11, comparing it with 2:12-17).

Our knowledge of God's love can have an effect on our choices and behaviour:

> Men and women who are made 'new' by the love of God are able to change the rules and the quality of relationships, transforming even social structures. They are people capable of bringing peace where there is conflict, of building and nurturing fraternal relationships where there is hatred, of seeking justice where there prevails the exploitation of man by man. (4)

Knowing that God is creator of all means that I can know that every person I meet along the path of my life is a fellow creature. Human beings are not mere accidents of nature; we are not specks of stellar dust in an infinite, unfeeling and unknowing universe; we are not mere cells in an organic collectivity; we are not just statistics in a set of economic calculations; we are not simply items of a population; we are not tiny elements in a vast political plan. (Nor are we tiny elements in a vast *divine* plan – we should not misunderstand references to God's 'plan', for example, in Chapter 1 of the *Compendium*, as in any way suggesting that human persons are merely puppets in a divine project or play. Human intelligence and free will are essential elements in God's plan.) Each person is meant to be because he or she has been deliberately created by God. Knowing that God is 'Our Father', to develop this theological perspective, means that I can know that everyone I meet, or can meet, is, at least potentially,[19] a brother or sister (in Christ) of mine. Knowing that Christ is Saviour, at least potentially, of all human persons means that everyone I can come into contact with, in whatever fashion, is someone that I might be spending eternity with in our home in heaven. Theological truths have social implications. No-one who truly believes in the Gospel and has made the commitment of living faith can look on others as total strangers to be ignored, or as 'others' to be feared and hated, or as enemies to be defeated or eliminated (see Mt 5:43-48 and 25:31-46). We must look at others with the eyes of Christ, with whom our living faith unites us, and see them as our neighbours, especially when they are in need and we can help them (see Lk 10:29-37).[20]

The effects of Christian faith, hope and love on how we look at other people, recognising their 'transcendent dignity' and our connection with them 'in a network of relationships', is a vast area to be explored. We have only begun to mention some aspects of it here. It is important to appreciate that theological truth can have a positive effect on all our dispositions and all our understanding, however, and not just in relation to 'religious' matters, or directly 'churchy' matters. In *Deus caritas est*, the Holy Father mentioned how faith can purify reason:

> From God's standpoint, faith liberates reason from its blind spots and therefore helps it to be ever more fully

> itself. Faith enables reason to do its work more effectively and to see its proper object more clearly. This is where Catholic social doctrine has its place: it has no intention of giving the Church power over the State. Even less is it an attempt to impose on those who do not share the faith ways of thinking and modes of conduct proper to faith. Its aim is simply to help purify reason and to contribute, here and now, to the acknowledgment and attainment of what is just.[21]

The final points mentioned in this quotation from Pope Benedict are important. It is essential that no one gets the idea that the Church claims to know everything about social matters and to have all the answers on economic, political and social problems. Far from it. The Church has clearly acknowledged that she does not have all the answers.[22] It should not be supposed that the Bible or Church documents, including the *Compendium*, or Catholic tradition in general cover the truths and principles of the natural or social sciences. One will not find out how to organise a modern economy by diligently studying the Bible; one will not get guidance in any detailed fashion from any Church document on how to run a government.[23]

Nevertheless, even though theology cannot answer all the important technical questions of politics and economics and science and other secular disciplines, it is vitally important not to exclude a theological perspective from politics, economics, science and other secular disciplines. As the quote from John Paul II that graces the title page of the first part of the *Compendium* puts it: 'The theological dimension is needed both for interpreting and for solving present day problems in human society.'[24] At the root of all social questions and problems lie 'essentially religious' questions about the meaning of the human person and our place in nature, and so on (see *Compendium*, 14–15). It is only with a correct understanding of the human person that we can understand our social problems and find adequate solutions to them. It is also necessary to have a correct understanding of the human person to avoid succumbing to inadequate and often very harmful 'solutions' to social problems. The Catholic Church offers her own members and also all of society the light of God's revelation to illuminate and purify our anthropology, ethics and politics. For example, the Christian understanding of sin and its various effects leads to an approach to solving social problems that is realistic and integral, avoiding, for example, the idea that a perfect set of political structures and leaders can reach any perfect solution for society's ills.[25] No society or set of social structures is perfect in this life, nor is any polity or politics beyond criticism and reform. An understanding of the human person *as precisely a person* is necessary if social action is not to end up demeaning people in what are perhaps good faith efforts to help them. One ought not to seek to solve social problems such as poverty and homelessness by focusing on only the physical needs of people, for example, or by treating people who are poor or homeless as mere victims to be pitied and kept in a state of dependence on social handouts. The principles of *subsidiarity* and *participation*, both of which are based on the dignity of the human person, which is clearly grasped in seeing every human being as created in the image of God, provide moral directives to guide individual, social and political action to help people who are poor or homeless in a way that respects their personhood in all its dimensions. And the principle of *solidarity* directs us never to ignore the needs of anyone.[26]

It is perhaps not too difficult to see how an understanding of the human person being created 'in the image of God'[27] can contribute greatly to our interpretation of social problems and to finding their solution, and much of what the *Compendium* contains is precisely the working out of what understanding the opening chapters of Genesis imply for anthropology, ethics and politics. However, there are other theological truths to be included in Catholic social doctrine too. Take, for example, the doctrine of the Trinity. One might be forgiven for thinking that such a doctrine is very much an otherworldly matter, a mystical reality that might interest those Christians who are attracted to the detached-from-this-world tendency outlined above, but of no relevance to social activists who are attached to temporal needs. There is a short section of the *Compendium* that offers a very positive and rewarding approach to understanding the doctrine of the Trinity in a way that is attractive and socially inspiring (see *Compendium,* 30–7). Understanding God as Trinity, insofar as one can understand a revealed mystery of such profundity, leads one to see that love is the most basic reality of all, precisely because God is love. God is not some majestic, lonely, infinite Being floating around in space, who decided to create a universe to take away his boredom and give him someone to talk to, to put it rather bluntly. No, Christian faith believes in a God who, though supremely one, is not a lonely isolated individual. God is a kind of community, we could say, if one is to be permitted to use colloquial language on this topic, but not a community that submerges the persons who constitute it into a personality-less collective, nor a community that lacks to any degree complete unity of being. In being Trinity, and in creating us in his image, God witnesses, in a sense, to the equal and primordial value of both individuality and community. A person is both an individual substance and a relationship; one is always to be understood as both distinctly oneself and in relationship to others. This leads to a rejection of any approach to social analysis and problem solving that relies on mere individualism (including over-emphasis on private property, for example) because such approaches neglect the essentially social nature of the human person; but it also leads to rejecting any collectivist 'solution' to social problems (that would abolish all private property, for example) because such collectivist approaches denigrate the dignity of the human person, who is never a mere means to an end, even good social end, but an end in himself or herself. The individuality and sociality of each and every human person is a dim but real reflection of the individuality and sociality of God, one God but three persons, three divine persons in the one God. Believing in the Trinity will not give us detailed answers to any social question, of course, but it will help us to see things in a wider and deeper perspective, and will help us to avoid errors of judgement and harmful policies and actions.

What has faith to do with politics? Hopefully, this brief look at only a few paragraphs from the *Compendium* helps to begin to answer this question. As seen in the *Compendium*'s opening paragraphs and indeed throughout its length, the Church's answer to what faith has to do with politics is: both everything and nothing. Which are we supposed to be, detached from or attached to this world and its concerns and needs? The Church answers: both detached and attached. What is to be our highest ideal, to love God or to love our neighbour as ourselves? The Church answers: both love commandments are obligatory and both are intrinsically linked. The two love commandments, which sum up the Ten Commandments and the whole law of Moses and the teachings of the Prophets (see Mt 22:34-40) are not contradictory, but complementary. Further, it could be said that the New Commandment of love, given by Jesus at the Last Supper both by exemplary deed and expository word,[28] sums up what Christian love specifically is. Christ's disciples are called to 'love one another as I have loved you', to love as Jesus Christ loved. As is expressed throughout all four gospels, Christ's love of us pervaded his life from beginning to end and beyond (see, for example, Mt 11:2-6, Mk 6:30-44, Lk 4:18-19, Jn 3:16-17). At the same time, everything Christ did was done for love of the Father and in accordance with the Father's will (see, for example, Mt 9:10-13, Mk 14:35-6, Lk 4:1-13, Jn 4:34). Loving us and loving the Father were not alternatives for Christ: he did both in all his actions. In so doing, he embodied both attachment to this world and its concerns and needs, in particular the concerns and needs of its people, and detachment from the world insofar as it is under the power of sin. His love for his friends was so great that he was prepared to lay down his life for them (see Jn 15:12-17). This love was expressed in many concrete ways in Jesus' life and ministry – in his Incarnation itself, in his living a loving family life for so many 'hidden' years, in his devotion to his Jewish faith, in his fearless preaching the truth, in his table fellowship with sinners and outcasts, in his healings and exorcisms, in his calling the Twelve and shaping them into a community, in his sanctification of marriage, in his blessing little children, in his challenging the status quo to change by accepting God's new covenant, in his non-violent acceptance of opposition and persecution and execution, in his courageous giving of himself in Sacrament and Cross. By loving men and women, Jesus loved the Father too; by loving the Father, he loved men and women. Jesus' love-of-God-by-love-of-man led directly to his crucifixion, which was the sacrifice that saves the world and its people, and God the Father ratified Jesus' loving sacrifice of himself, a sacrifice that embodied both Jesus' supreme attachment to his friends and his utter detachment from sin and sinfulness, by raising Jesus from the dead, and so hope for a new creation and a new life was born.

Love of people and their concerns and needs is expressed not only in personal or private choices and acts, but also in political choices and acts. Love is the moral ideal that we are called to always respect and live by. Thus, politics can embody a proper attachment to this world insofar as it embodies love for our neighbours and our world. Faith calls us to love in this way, to be attached to our neighbour and our world – love necessitates *attachment*. Our faith calls us also to love God directly, we could say, by various religious activities, many of which embody a critical attitude to this world and its temptations and distractions. Thus, faith embodies detachment from this world – love necessitates *detachment*. But the attachment and the detachment called for by our Christian faith and love are intrinsically interlinked. Though we are called to be detached from sin and temptation and distraction, we are not called to be detached from the people who are made in God's image, nor from the world insofar as it is God's good creation, a creation that is redeemed and called to fulfilment in Christ. Though we are directed to be attached to this world and its people insofar as they are God's creation, we are not called to be so attached to worldly concerns and needs that we forget our calling to a transcendent destiny, a destiny that calls us away from selfishness and narrowness and mere worldliness to a love and life that shares in the very love and life of the Ultimate Reality, the Holy Trinity, the God who is creative and redeeming love.

Notes

1 Cf. John Paul II, *Fides et Ratio* 41. Church documents are usually available in full online and are most easily accessed by using a search engine such as Google. Quotations here are taken from the Vatican website: www.vatican.va.

2 These images should not be taken to mean that faith is fully expressed by reference to the Holy See, the Vatican or Archbishop's House; nor is politics fully exemplified by the UN, Washington DC, Brussels or Leinster House. Both faith and politics are much broader realities than these images suggest, and can involve all people, at various levels of activity, and not just religious or political leaders.

3 As usual with Church documents, all references are to paragraph numbers rather than pages (except when referring to the indexes). The edition of the *Compendium of the Social Doctrine of the Church* (or *Compendium* for short) used here is: Vatican: Liberia Editrice Vaticana, 2004. This *Compendium* (on Social Doctrine) is not to be confused with another compendium of Catholic doctrine recently published, the *Compendium of the Catechism of the Catholic Church.*

4 Although there is no space to go into it in any detail here, it is worth noting that there is a genuine and legitimate pluralism in the Church on exactly where the emphasis should be put in finding the middle ground between detachment and attachment. Even though there is agreement on rejecting the extreme answers, Christians do not always agree on details as to where in the middle the correct answer is to be found.

5 For an accessible and provocative account of how monastic and social activist types of Christian practice have contributed

greatly to the Church and to western society, see T.E. Woods, *How the Catholic Church Built Western Civilization*, Washington DC, Regnery, 2005, particularly chapters 3 (monasticism), 7 (international law), 8 (economics), 9 (charity) and 10 (western law).

6 This phrase is taken from the well-known traditional prayer, the Hail Holy Queen.

7 This quote is from the popular modern hymn 'City of God' by Fr Dan Schutte, S.J.

8 It was passages such as these that inspired Tertullian's dismissal of philosophy as incompatible with faith.

9 I deal in some detail with the scriptural and traditional grounding for the Judeo-Christian vision of justice and peace in my book, *Issues of Justice and Peace*, *Into the Classroom* series, Dublin, Veritas, 2005. The *Compendium* was published just as my book was being finished so, unfortunately, I was unable to integrate its insights and approach directly into my own work.

10 See Pope Benedict XVI, *Deus caritas est*, 20–6. This encyclical as a whole offers a brilliant answer to the questions examined here. For a detailed historical survey of the teaching and activity of the Church concerning social action and justice, see Roger Charles, *Christian Social Witness and Teaching: The Catholic Tradition from Genesis to Centesimus Annus*, Vols. 1 and 2, Herefordshire, Gracewing, 1998.

11 Although the section on the family does not have the title 'Biblical Aspects' as the other sections do, it does have a short section devoted to the biblical grounds for Church thinking on the family: see *Compendium*, 209–11. It is worth noting too that the chapter on human rights has many references to biblical passages that speak of human dignity and the nature of the human person.

12 It should be noted that the term 'politics' is used here in its broadest sense, rather than in the narrower sense confined to party politics and elections (see note 2 above). Politics in its broadest sense refers to a whole range of institutions and structures that organise power in society. See *Issues of Justice and Peace*, pp. 43–6, 53–61.

13 Hopefully, readers will not be put off by this rather forbidding use of terminology in the very beginning of the *Compendium*.

One challenge facing the Church is to find accessible language to present its teachings to all. Actually, most parts of the *Compendium* are quite accessible, although its length might be somewhat off-putting, especially to the beginner. Therefore, it might be advisable to begin with an introductory book such as K. Himes, *Responses to 101 Questions and Answers on Catholic Social Teaching*, Paulist Press, 2001, or R. Charles, *An Introduction to Catholic Social Teaching*, Ignatius Press, 2000. Such books, however, do not substitute for the *Compendium* itself.

14 The internal quotation is from *Redemptoris Missio*, the 1991 encyclical of John Paul II on missionary work. John Paul's teachings are a major influence on the *Compendium*, and are frequently quoted, as can readily be seen by looking at the index of references, 345–51, (the longest listing of any single source other than the Bible itself).

15 This phrase is taken from the first paragraph of the *Compendium*. The whole paragraph is thoroughly Christocentric.

16 Emphasis is in the original. The internal quote is taken from the *Catechism of the Catholic Church*, 2419.

17 The generic 'man' is useful as it can refer to both human persons, male and female, but also Christ, who, although he was not a human person, was fully 'a man' and 'man'. In bearing witness to 'man', the Church bears witness simultaneously to both Christ and the human person. Perhaps this is one reason the term 'man' is used in official Church texts, even though such language runs the serious risk of being the occasion, if not the cause, of misunderstanding and offence. Such language is not meant to be understood in any way as exclusive of women, and makes no real sense if read that way. Misunderstandings of such generic use are avoided when other cognate expressions, such as 'human persons', are sometimes used as well as the generic 'man', as is done often in the *Compendium*. However, consistently substituting 'human person' for 'man' does not facilitate the close parallel with Christ, which is so central to Christian faith and to the rationale of Catholic social doctrine, because Christ, though fully 'man', was and is a divine person, not a human person, strictly speaking. See *Catechism of the Catholic Church*, 456–83.

18 That 'God is love' is the central theme of Pope Benedict XVI's first encyclical, an encyclical that bears that very title, and this underlines its importance as a Christian doctrine.

19 The issue of distinguishing between those who are explicitly in God's family, the Church, and those who are called to be in it, and might be implicitly in it even now, is too vast a topic to look at here. (The issue is not dealt with fully in the *Compendium*, as far as I can see, but see pars. 39 and 41 for hints at a resolution of the problem.) The modern approach of the Church towards those who are not explicitly Catholics is outlined briefly in the Vatican II Dogmatic Constitution on the Church, *Lumen Gentium*, 13–16 (especially 16).

20 Interestingly, the third section of the *Catechism of the Catholic Church*, the one on morality, is called 'Life In Christ'. This very title is a good summary of what Christian morality is all about. On seeing with the eyes of Christ, see *Deus caritas est*, 18.

21 *Deus caritas est*, 28.

22 See Vatican II, *Gaudium et spes* (Pastoral Constitution on the Church in the Modern World), 36, 43. Of course, it does not follow that, because the Church does not claim to have all the answers to social problems, therefore she has none. It is not a matter of all or nothing (as this whole chapter is arguing).

23 The *Compendium* mentions several times that Church social doctrine is constantly to be in dialogue with other forms of human knowledge, always respectful of the proper autonomy of the various 'spheres' that make up the whole of our personal and political activity: see 8, 18, 50, and especially 72–8.

24 The quote is taken from *Centesimus annus*, the 1991 social encyclical that marked the hundredth anniversary of Pope Leo XIII's encyclical *Rerum Novarum*, the encyclical that started off the modern phase of Catholic social doctrine. See *Compendium* 87–103 for a concise outline of the modern history of papal teachings in this area.

25 Catholic social doctrine is very much against any form of totalitarianism and it allows for political use of coercion or violence only in very restricted circumstances (which exclude any deliberate and direct attacks on non-combatants). See the *Compendium* index under the headings 'totalitarianism' and 'war' for specific references.

26 These principles, subsidiarity, participation and solidarity, are treated in Chapter 4 of the *Compendium*, and underlie, with the other principles treated in that chapter, the whole of the applied directives presented in the second part of the *Compendium*.

27 For more on this topic, see *Compendium*, Chapter 3, Section II, and the anthropology developed in section III.

28 See Jn 13:1-16 for the washing of the disciples' feet, and Jn 13:34 for the wording of the commandment.

5

THE COMMON GOOD IN AN UNEQUAL WORLD

An Taoiseach Bertie Ahern

I note that the *Allegory of Good Government*, from the Civic Palace in Siena, was chosen to illustrate the Compendium. I have always been interested in the fact that the Council of Siena met under that beautiful but stern reminder of the consequences for citizens of the decisions that they made.

In my own experience citizens are far more likely to reflect the message about bad government also portrayed in that room, by blaming the government even for bad weather and poor sports results, without giving us any credit when things go well! Nonetheless, the message to governments remains clear: to govern well, choose justice and act justly by seeking wisdom. The wisdom to be found in the social teaching contained in the *Compendium* is both ancient and modern. It is ancient because it draws on the insight into the nature of the human person found in Scripture and the spiritual tradition of the Church over centuries. It is modern, in that the expression of its application to life today is to be found in the great documents of the popes addressing contemporary issues. This begins with *Rerum Novarum* of Pope Leo XIII. That document dealt with the very pressing contemporary question of labour and its rights within a just social order. That essential message about the requirements to be met for the common good was restated at critical points, such as by Pius XI in the fact of international financial crisis and the rise of totalitarian regimes during the 1930s. Blessed John XXIII addressed the 'Signs of the Times', regarding the increasingly global challenge of development. He positioned the Church as a cooperator in building up, with all men and women, an authentic economic development which would promote their dignity. In the fact of nuclear proliferation and the risk of nuclear conflict, he addressed 'all men of goodwill' on the challenge faced by the world community to develop systems to promote the universal common good.

The Second Vatican Council in its great Pastoral Constitution of the Church asserted the importance and relevance of its social message. It also asserted the central importance of its pastoral concern for the problems of men and women and for dialogue with the world. Later, Paul VI expressed a profound truth when he wrote that 'development is the new name for peace'. His vision of a 'complete humanism' inspired by spiritual values struck a chord which resonates even today. In his writing, the late John Paul II returned to the theme of work and its importance for the dignity of every person and as a foundation for a just social life. Writing in the context of the collapse of the Soviet system, John Paul asserted the critical importance of social solidarity, if the values of democracy and the free economy are truly to provide a basis for authentic human development.

This important volume, drawing together the insights from this tradition, is therefore not only of value to members of the Catholic Church, it is also of value to all people of goodwill who would seek to develop their understanding and to build right relationships between peoples. The world today is acutely in need of such wonderfully positive expressions of faith and guidance to assist us in difficult times. It would be difficult for the ordinary person, coping with the many distractions of modern living, to find time to explore all the source materials covered in the *Compendium*. Yet I do not doubt that many people will dedicate time to this volume and find it a rewarding and fulfilling experience.

While religious faith and practice have declined, or at least find less obvious expression in the Church, the spiritual dimension remains vital in the lives of most people. The ethical principles of the Judaeo-Christian tradition have shaped our society and culture. They are central to how we see ourselves as a nation and to our vision of the wider world. Developing over centuries, Christian teaching has been the cornerstone for the cultural development of Europe. In Ireland, our personal and national responses to the great public issues have been informed by these principles. This tradition of faith and values remains central to most of us as we contemplate the ultimate questions of who we are and the meaning of our existence. My own experience in government convinces me of the continued importance of these principles. If I were to focus on one thing that has been at the centre of my political vision, it is the dignity of the human person. Whether seeking advances in the economic and social conditions in the state, building improved relationships on the island of Ireland, engaging in closer partnerships in Europe or addressing our national responsibilities towards global needs and targets, I have sought to maintain a central focus on the effects of decisions on the lives of individual people, today and in the future.

The emphasis in Catholic social teaching on the rights of labour is, to me, one of its most attractive features. When it was, in many quarters, deeply unpopular to say so, the Church asserted that trade unions were an indispensable element of social life. It saw them as promoters of the struggle for social justice and for the rights of workers, rather than against others. With great foresight, this teaching saw trade unions as having a role beyond the defence of the interests of members, by having a role in working for 'the proper arrangement of economic life and of educating the social consciences of workers'(307). As such, this teaching sees workers' representatives as having responsibilities in regard to the production of wealth and the creation of the social, political and cultural conditions that permit all to exercise their right to work with dignity. That teaching was, and is, accompanied by a focus on the rights of property and of those who own and manage businesses, accepting the proper role of profit as the first indicator that a business is functioning well. The support given to the free market as an institution reflects its social importance in bringing about effective results in the production of goods and services and, thus, as an effective instrument for attaining important objectives of justice. The Church teaches, however, that no economic system can be entirely free, and sustainable, at the same time: it must be firmly rooted in ethical objectives, which ensure the achievement of solidarity and the defence of the weak.

There is much in Irish policy and public life which reflects the wisdom of those insights. I would cite, for example, the critical importance to the quality of our society, and to the dignity of the life of individual citizens, of the economic development which has brought about a dramatic increase in the number of people at work. I believe passionately that access to work of good quality, and with good conditions, is central to peace, stability and development. The transformation of Ireland from a land of emigration and unemployment to one of immigration and virtually full employment is, for me, the most satisfying of the achievements of modern Ireland. That achievement has been significantly facilitated by the development of a spirit of social partnership between government, trade unions, employers, farm organisations and the wider voluntary sector of civil society. In line with the principles reflected in this *Compendium*, each of these players has recognised the legitimate interests and responsibilities of the others. Ways have been developed to facilitate the achievement of shared objectives, while respecting the fundamental differences which remain between the interests and goals of each interest. The government, for its part, has recognised the value of listening carefully to the insights and experiences of the social partners, and recognising our capacity to achieve most when the policy environment reflects their input.

I subscribe strongly to the importance of the concept of the common good as 'the sum total of social conditions which allow people, either as groups or as individuals, to reach their fulfilment more fully or more easily' (164). This has been at the heart of the partnership model of economic planning that has been employed successfully in recent decades. We live in a society which is progressing rapidly in material wealth and educational attainment. At the same time, our purpose has been to improve services and support for those in greater need or less able to manage independently. I believe that the Irish people share a vision of an inclusive, inter-dependent and caring society. The principles of subsidiarity and solidarity are fundamental to our domestic administration and international relations. Solidarity is the bedrock of the success of the European Union. After our accession to the EU, we benefited hugely from the financial support of the richer member states. Now that we ourselves are among the more prosperous member states, we fully accept that we should support the efforts of our new partners in Central and Eastern Europe to develop their economic and social systems. This means that Ireland will gradually become a net contributor to the budget of the EU. This is as it should be. We will show the same solidarity to the new member states that we ourselves received.

In the wider international arena, I have, personally, always been strongly committed to solidarity among nations, and between the rich and the poor. It is quite simply morally and ethically unacceptable that over a billion of our fellow human beings should live in conditions of absolute poverty, subsisting on less than $1 per day. I think, on the basis of our own history, and of the immense contribution our missionaries have made to development, that we in Ireland have a special sense of solidarity with the poorest of the poor. There is, therefore, widespread public support for the government's efforts to increase our national development assistance budget. This will reach .7% of our GNP by 2012. This year, we will spend €675 million on ODA. Our aid budget will reach .5% of our GNP in 2007. This is indeed a very concrete expression of our solidarity with the poor, and funds an aid programme that is internationally recognised for its effectiveness and its focus on meeting basic needs.

Subsidiarity is an important principle, both in the life of the Church and in the wider world. In the European Union, subsidiarity is one of the fundamental guiding principles of the Union. It is given concrete expression in the draft European Constitution. In a complex multilateral body such as the EU, where member states have voluntarily pooled national sovereignty in certain areas in order to achieve common objectives, it is important that the centralising forces of bureaucracy are counterbalanced by the stringent application of the principles of subsidiarity and proportionality.

The emphasis in this *Compendium* on the importance of political involvement in the democratic process, I find particularly welcome and challenging. The clear assertion of the value of a system that ensures the participation of citizens in making political choices, that guarantees to the governed the possibility both of electing and holding accountable those who govern them, and of replacing them through peaceful means, is an important statement of the ethical importance of politics and the democratic process. In a very clear expression of the proper separation of Church and State, the Second Vatican Council solemnly affirmed that the political community and the Church are mutually independent and self-governing. That is not to imply a form of separation that requires distance or excludes cooperation. The Church argues that the good of all is best achieved if Church and State work better, for wholesome mutual cooperation, in a way suitable to the circumstances of time and place.

It is in that spirit that the draft European Constitutional Treaty provides for a structured dialogue with the Churches, faith communities and non-confessional bodies. In that same spirit, the Irish government decided to initiate such a process of dialogue at the domestic level. I am pleased to say that the response has been strongly positive. Detailed arrangements for the initiation of such dialogue on the basis of principles adopted by the government, following consultation with the Churches, are at an advanced stage. I believe that it provides an important framework within which the values expressed in this

Compendium can be discussed and applied. I welcome all initiatives that enrich debate about the quality of life and the development of greater citizen participation in our society. A political community is healthy if it enjoys the committed loyalty of its citizens, rather than merely requiring their compliance with rules. In the words of the *Compendium*:

> An authentic democracy is not merely the result of a formal observation of a set of rules, but is the fruit of a convinced acceptance of the values that inspire democratic procedures: the dignity of every human person, the respect of human rights, and commitment to the common good as the purpose and guiding criterion for political life. (407)

Study and reflection on the contents of this important volume will, I believe, contribute to the attainment of that committed engagement on the part of members of the Church and other people of goodwill.

6

THOUGHTS ON THE *COMPENDIUM*: Challenges of the Twenty-First Century

Lord Chris Patten

If I begin with a few fragments of my personal history, it is not because vanity insists on padding out but to help explain the point of take-off for my argument. I am a retired Conservative politician, a Catholic and a British passport holder. Like millions of other British citizens I am partly Irish, the great-grandson of potato famine migrants, the grandson of Catholic head-teachers in the Manchester slums who began teaching before the 1902 Balfour Act allowed them to be paid from the public purse. My Irish forebears would, I dare say, have been surprised to learn that their offspring had the task of closing down the British empire. So I am a good working example of the nonsense of thinking that we can deal with the world's problems on the basis of pure-blooded, simple tribal loyalties and identities. Yet much of my political career has been spent dealing with a world inhabited by those who asserted exactly the opposite. On this island, for example, I have been one of those who had to cope with the consequences of this belief. And yet what does the name Adams tell you about his tribe or the name Molyneux about his for that matter? It was not only in Northern Ireland that I confronted the assumption that the world is divided into rigid castes. Working as a European Commissioner in the blood-stained Balkans, I dealt with the same sort of legacy of tribal hate. It finds its worst expression in nationalist extremism. Our Church has to be careful about the importance of keeping its distance from this revanchism – in Croatia for example.

Nationalism tore Europe apart in the first half of the last century. So after the Second World War, we framed a political order for ourselves, encouraged by American post-war diplomacy, in which we turned our back on the politics of the nineteenth century, and tried to shape a political culture in which you can be a patriot without being a nationalist. We recognised that the nation state is the largest entity to which people feel a natural loyalty, and yet we also recognised that nation states need to work together to a unique extent to provide the security and prosperity that their citizens require and expect. Globalisation renders porous the boundaries of nation states. We live in a world where the Catholic Church, both because of the nature of its mission, above and beyond political frontiers, and because of its institutional structure, should feel very much at home. The Church understands, to quote from the *Compendium of the Social Doctrine,* that human beings 'are living members of the whole human family'. At one level, the Church certainly demonstrates that it *is* at home – taking its message to favelas in Latin America, to townships in South Africa and to the sprawling cities of Asia. I have seen the Church at work in all these environments. It is inspiring. But at another level, and perhaps this is an inevitable reflection of the Church's understanding of human frailty, it can give the impression that this is a world that it wants to get off. It is, of course, the only world we've got; it is not in my view a worse place than the one I was born into sixty years ago. I grew to adulthood in a world where an uneasy peace was maintained because of the mutual fear on the part of the antagonists of East and West of what would happen if the cold war suddenly went hot. Peace was preserved for most of us because the alternative was nuclear conflagration. I have lived through decades when millions starved in Asia as well as in Africa, when economic opportunity seemed confined to the few, when their gender condemned women in most countries to at best a second- or third-class existence of drudgery, ignorance and discrimination. We face some terrible problems today, but we do so from a little higher up the ladder.

What is more, while some regard me as a Pollyanna, I believe those problems are soluble given the resources, the leadership and the will. Are we to respond to those challenges in the most powerful and prosperous nations by retreating behind our own walls and our own security guards like the inhabitants of a rich suburb, lashing out occasionally at the manifestations beyond our gated community of a dark Hobbesian horror show? Or do we go out from our redoubt generously and boldly to try to make things better, refusing to accept the idea that the world is simply a barbaric Darwinian battlefield?

How does the social teaching of the Catholic Church respond to the prospects faced by the citizens of the twenty-first century? How, in the words of Cardinal Sodano, can we learn to deal with temporal affairs according to God's will? There is a real problem of language here, of the narrative offered by the Church. The lilies of the field neither toil nor spin, so one should not confuse Catholic social teaching with a political manifesto. What would a Catholic macro-economic policy be? It would presumably advocate high employment, social solidarity – in other words generous social welfare, encouragement of enterprise and (I would hope) low inflation. This does not frankly get us very far and, certainly for a British taste, the attempts to translate this social teaching too literally into political programmes (for example on the part of European Christian Democrat parties in the past) produced a mixture of pretty vacuous waffle and rather old-fashioned dirigisme. This dwelt unhappily alongside the Church's enthusiasm for subsidiarity, a good principle of Catholic action insufficiently practised by governments in most European countries. The concept of subsidiarity, a bad word for the principle that lies at the heart of what the *Compendium* calls 'the realm of civil society', has been one of the Church's most important contributions to modern notions of good governance. But maybe all this slightly misses the point. Lay Catholics do not presumably want from their Church a blueprint for political action but an intellectual framework that shows the relevance of their religious beliefs to their everyday lives. They want a statement that reflects the spiritual messages of the Church, and which can provide them with assistance in working out for themselves how to cope with the real world's problems and opportunities. It offers them more than a few fingerprints or clues, but does not usually give them precise answers to day-to-day questions. Politics and morality are not the same, though we would all hope that the former is influenced by the latter. But Church and State are and should remain separate.

I was struck the other day by a newspaper report that young people these days live more and more without a watch strapped around their wrists. I have had a watch ever since my first Holy Communion. Except when I have been in hospital I doubt there has been a day when I have not worn a watch. I put it on when I get up in the morning and take it off at night. Without it, I would be slightly panicked. I would know without looking that I was not wearing it. So what do the watchless young do? Check their mobile phones apparently. What more do you need? Now this change of fashion does not change the nature of Time itself. There are still sixty minutes to the hour and twenty-four hours to the day. But our relationship to time is clearly changing. So there is no requirement to alter what is fundamental to one's beliefs, as fundamental in its way as the nature of Time, even while you seek to relate those beliefs to a world that has changed at a phenomenal pace and where change continues to accelerate.

The century that we have just survived saw the end of empire – British, Russian, Ottoman, French, Portuguese, Austro-Hungarian, American. It has seen the triumph of self-determination – Woodrow Wilson trumped Lenin. Though globalisation is no longer as fashionable an idea as it was, this implacable phenomenon is unstoppable. It is a result of peace, technology and the opening of market places under a set of international rules. This increasingly inter-dependent world has lived latterly under the Pax Americana. For their part, European countries have shared sovereignty in a unique if occasionally ramshackle way which now covers most of the continent: the wonder being what we do together, not what we argue about or fail to do. We are collectively better off around the world than the majority of us would ever have imagined possible, and most of us live in countries that are more or less democratic – in which there is at least participation in government if not always the rule of law. Democratisation has consequences for the Church, of course. In democracies, authority is not blindly accepted; it is often regarded with suspicion and it usually has to be earned. Attempts to impose authority provoke hostility and trigger alienation. This rubs off on governance within the Church and also on the role of those who articulate the Church's message, explaining it to the laity. While noting once again that the Church is not a political institution, this new attitude to hierarchy and civil relations is bound to affect attitudes in every walk of life. The Church should not feel uncomfortable about this, nor that it is being 'targeted'. Authority, humbly exercised, earns trust and affection, a point which the Church knows well. There is another sense in which the sort of world order, advocated rightly by the Church, has consequences for the Church itself. Transparency in government and a proper regard for human rights are advocated by priests and bishops. We want governments to tell the truth about what they do. We want them to respect the human rights of their citizens. Archbishop Romero is only one of the courageous Catholics who have died for these principles. The situation within the institutional Church is not precisely the same as that in a nation state, but some of the same considerations apply. To make a point that is alas more germane in some places than we would like it to be, openness even at the risk of embarrassment is always the best policy.

How should the Church deal with globalisation? Not, for a start, by trying to prevent it or hold it back, even if that was possible. On the whole, globalisation in the last few years has helped to lift many millions out of poverty, especially in China and India. The problem is that while many have been helped, too many have been left behind. Over a billion men, women and children still subsist on less than a dollar a day. Too many children die before their fifth birthday. Too many children – especially girls – are not taught to read and write. Too many are killed by epidemic disease. Too many lack clean drinking water. The Church has been an important part of the lobby in developed countries to devote more aid to the poor, and in particular to make clear and substantial progress towards meeting the UN's Millennium Development Goals. And Catholic aid agencies are active on the ground in the poorest and harshest places in the world, seeking to alleviate the conditions there. I was glad that Pope Benedict referred to this work in his encyclical on love [*Deus caritas est*] and that he noted that this developmental work was good in itself and should not be regarded as a way of converting the poor through meeting some of their material needs.

This is, I believe, an area where the Church can and should be even more outspoken. As a former political target of development lobbyists – as Britain's Development Minister in the 1980s – it seems to me that the subject is so important that one should not be too diplomatic or restrained in the way that the case for greater equity in the world is argued. It is not only a matter of aid, but of course of trade too. This is a difficult subject to broach in a country where agriculture is such an important part of the economy. But frankly the EU's Common Agricultural Policy is difficult to defend if you believe that the world's economic rules should be fair for all. Poorer countries are more likely to depend on their agriculture than richer ones. While it is true that we give the very poorest relatively open access to our markets, there is little excuse for protecting our farmers behind a wall of high tariffs. Where would the CAP today fit in to Catholic social teaching? In France, the greatest CAP beneficiary, 1 per cent of the largest farms receive more than the total amount that goes to the smallest 40 per cent. I dare say that the pattern is similar in Britain and Ireland. This highlights one substantial difference between the globalisation so well described by J.M. Keynes that swept the world in the late-nineteenth century and up to the First World War. Then, we saw the open movement of money, goods, food and people.

Today, the rich are keen on the free movement of goods and money but we have largely constrained free movement of food and people. We are protectionist about our food producers and scared of migrants. One result of keeping out food is to increase the number of illegal migrants from poor countries. If they cannot find work in their own countries, for example growing crops, they seek work legally or illegally in ours.

Of course, we should not regard economic growth in rich countries as a bad thing. In a literal sense it makes us more prone to consumerism, quite simply because there is more to consume and we have more money to spend on consumer goods and services. But there is a wealth of evidence that countries that prosper are more generous and tolerant to their minorities and to other groups of outsiders than those that do not. Economic hardship too frequently prompts people to look for scapegoats. They invariably target migrants and smaller ethnic groups. Growth in itself – becoming better off – is not therefore a bad thing, and we should not assume that because people in a growing economy have more money in their pockets and more leisure, they will inevitably become more selfish, thoughtless and materialistic. A higher standard of living does not necessarily imply a lower quality of life, though it can certainly do so. So I hope that the Church, whatever its legitimate criticisms of a barren consumerist culture, will not sound as though it wants to turn the clock back to the days before televisions and washing machines. There is a more valid critique of growth with which the Church should identify itself. I hope it will do so not least because of the personal outlook of Pope Benedict, who clearly cares about our threatened environment. The *Compendium* is admirably comprehensive on this subject. The argument that growth should be sustainable is not just a slogan. At a time when some think we may already have reached the tipping point in relation to global warming and climate change, the Church should help lead and shape the debate on protecting our environment against further degradation. An American senator recently argued that perhaps one way of convincing President

Bush of the importance of environmental issues was by pointing out to him that the earth was in a way a faith-based initiative! There really is an ethical issue here – how we preserve the global commons and hand them on to a new generation in good condition. We are custodians of our planet, not its reckless masters, a point that increasingly reflects expedience as well as morality. I was reading the other day some comments by the Solidarity hero of the Polish revolution, Lech Walesa. Discussing the end of Communism in Europe, he assigned 50 per cent of the credit to the Polish pope. Some might contest the precise percentage awarded to John Paul II, but few surely would deny the central role he played in redrawing the political geography of Europe.

But what of the way we organise our lives, the choices we make for example about marriage and family? In Europe we appear to have moved from baby boom to baby bust in one generation. Fertility rates have dropped from well over the replacement rate of 2.1 children per woman in the 1960s to well below. In a number of countries the average age of a mother at the birth of her first child has risen sharply, for example in Italy from 25.7 in 1961 to 30.4 in 2001. This is a global issue, not simply one facing 'old Europe'. Wherever in the world there is a reasonable level of prosperity, a high level of female literacy and a cheap and safe supply of contraceptives, used without moral stigma, the birth rate falls below the replacement level of two. The figures in secular Islamic Turkey, Shi'ite Iran and Catholic Brazil are all forecast to fall below that level in the next fifteen years. Let me mention some of the obvious results in Europe. Average household size is in decline – from 2.9 to 2.4 people since 1971 in Britain and from 3.3 to 2.6 in the same period in Italy. The EU's population will be falling over the first half of this century – by 22 per cent in Italy, 15 per cent in Poland and 8 per cent in Spain. These figures, don't forget, are the result of the choices that individuals make. We cannot force families to have more children. Nor is the answer to try to drive women back to the traditional role from which they have been escaping. Indeed, there is a good deal of evidence that the developed countries that enjoy the highest birth rates are those where women enjoy the greatest economic freedom. At the same time that we will be seeing in Europe a 20 per cent decline in the size of our working age population, the median age will be rising dramatically by almost twelve years over the next fifty. So fewer people in work will have to support more people out of work. This is bound to lead to more women being encouraged to join the labour market, for example in Italy, where at present only four in ten females are in employment.

The causes and the implications of these dramatic demographic shifts need to be debated by our Church as well as by our political leaders. It is inevitable, and not unreasonable, that many will contrast what has happened to Europe's politics, to the historic boundaries of our continent, with what has happened in so many European families. Perhaps it is easier for us to see some other family issues in the context of social policy, ignorance and poverty. Does the absence of the provision of good healthcare, regardless of need, and of responsible sex education have at least something to do with the fact that American girls (according to former President Jimmy Carter, a devout Christian) 'are five times as likely to have a baby as French girls, seven times as likely to have an abortion and seventy times as likely to have gonorrhoea as girls in the Netherlands'. American teenagers are five times as likely to suffer from HIV/AIDS as Germans. I fear that Britain would not come as well as some other European countries out of these comparisons. So the explanation for these grisly figures cannot relate entirely to prosperity, free health care and health education. On the other hand, the social context of personal behaviour must play a greater part in explaining why, according to the UN, four million abortions, most of them illegal, take place in Latin America annually with up to 5,000 women dying from complications resulting from abortions. A pro-life policy should also be a pro-welfare and pro-health education policy, even if those things are not nearly enough.

I have already mentioned economic globalisation, its potentially boundless opportunities and some of its unfairnesses. There is a dark side of globalisation – threats that are magnified and expedited by modern technology and practices. A disease that might once have taken decades or even centuries to span the world can now threaten us all in years or months. Consider HIV/AIDS or Avian influenza. The drug trade, organised crime, trafficking in children and young women are other grim examples of this negative side of globalisation. The proliferation of nuclear weapons, with North Korea and Iran the present focuses of international concern, should join the list. What might a rational citizen conclude? Surely that our existing institutionalised efforts at international cooperation, based on the United Nations, need to go much further. This is no time to argue that authority to act politically should lie primarily or mainly with nation states. The notion of subsidiarity advocates devolving power to the appropriate level for decision-taking. We need to consider the opposite need, pushing power to take decisions up to the level required if they are to unlock the sort of action that could deal with the problems that threaten us. Sadly the attempts to reform and strengthen the UN last autumn achieved all too little. But practical experience as well as aspiration underline how important this work is. It may seem counter-intuitive when we look at the mayhem and murder in Colombia, West Africa, Sudan or Iraq, but actually the number of conflicts around the world has fallen in the last fifteen years and so has the number of casualties resulting from them. Why? Partly because, believe it or not, we have become better at preventing and ending conflict, and at the heart of those endeavours have been pro-active diplomacy and the UN. For one consequence of this, look at the number of Irish troops involved in peace-keeping around the world.

There is one further issue that I want to raise in which the Church already plays a constructive and helpful role: that is the relationship with the Islamic world. A decade ago, an American political scientist Samuel Huntington wrote first an essay and then a book arguing that, just when some might think we were entering a war-free world, we were actually going to be confronted by a clash of civilizations. At the time, most of the debate engendered by this proposition concentrated on the alleged conflict of values between Confucian and Western societies; Huntington's argument became an excuse for denying democracy, human rights and the rule of law to East Asians. Today, the argument is most sharply joined in relation to the West (Europe and America) and the Islamic world, bearing in mind of course that some of that Islamic world is (as it has been for much of our history) here in Europe. Terrorism gives the subject a sharp edge. President Bush defines the enemy in America's 'war on terrorism' as 'radical Islam'. I put on one side for the time being the fact there is not in my judgement a 'war' on terrorism, as there were wars between knightly states, between nation states and between industrial societies. What there is is a continuing use of violence against liberal, open societies for political ends. But I won't dwell on that important point. It is the description of 'the enemy' that I want to focus on.

Our knowledge of Islam is weak. We do know, however, that you can distinguish between political, missionary and jihadist Islam. It is the last of those groups that condones and nurtures terrorism. Political Islam may be radical, but it does not necessarily collude with terrorism, and if we are going to argue that the spread of democracy and the institutions associated with it in an open society is the answer to jihadism we will have to deal with this political Islam. I have already mentioned the hugely important and influential role that the Church can play in promoting dialogue with the Islamic world and advancing the understanding of it. There are perhaps three rather political or sociological issues that the dialogue I am sure will incorporate. First, Moslems do not have a completely different set of values to those non-Moslems who live in Europe and America. All the polling evidence suggests a remarkable similarity of values. We might also remember that three-quarters of the world's Moslems live outside the Middle East and North Africa, many of them in functioning democratic societies in Asia like India, Malaysia and Indonesia. Second, we must be careful to explain that it is rarely the televised extremists who represent their faith and their societies, though they are often manipulated by repressive and unpopular governments as though they did, something that has clearly happened during the row over the notorious Danish cartoons. Third, we can use our experience and voice to accommodate Moslems to the Enlightenment values that predominate in our own societies in Europe, which bear the stamp of Voltaire, Locke and John Stuart Mill. Historically the Enlightenment challenged the Catholic Church. Blasphemy and heresy no longer bring down on the heads of the perpetrators civil as well as religious sanctions. So we have long since learned to live in a world which recognises the difference between liberty and licence, but sensibly usually leaves personal judgement and choice to police this distinction. Our civilization depends above all on our behaviour as individuals on the choices we make.

To go back for a moment to that disagreeable controversy over the cartoons, we believe in freedom of speech but expect (alas, we are often disappointed) that it will be exercised in ways that do not hurt or insult. It is not to resile from our secular Enlightenment values to argue that freedom of speech should accommodate respect for other cultures and religions. But people who belong to other religions or civilizations should understand those values, even if they do not like them. They should not use their rejection of them to try to impose their extremist view of their own religion on their communities.

I hope this has not been too breathless, superficial or provocative a *tour d'horizon*. The fact that I have ranged so wide reflects the breadth of the Church's own role and mission in the flawed world of man. The message of the Church is delivered to the faithful in a building constructed, inevitably, out of the 'crooked timber of humanity'. No one is more challenged by the consequences of humanity's imperfectability than those with a vocation to save its souls.

SECTION THREE

Solidarity and Freedom

7

A SHARED HUMANISM BASED ON SOLIDARITY: Principles for Reflection, Criteria for Judgement and Guidelines for Action

Archbishop Diarmuid Martin

It is important to remember at the outset that the *Compendium of the Social Doctrine of the Church* is not a recipe book with ready-made answers to the social, political, economic and cultural questions of the times. It presents a unified corpus of principles and criteria which draw their origin from the gospels and which are applied to the realities of the times in order to form Christians to make their own responsible contribution to the dialogue between the Gospel and modern culture. Catholic social teaching is not an ideology. The Christian is not some sort of robot programmed by a book of social doctrine. The *Compendium* presupposes the subjectivity and responsibility of each human person and that the individual – rich or poor – is able to express fundamental human liberty in the economic and social field. It is above all an instrument to guide the formation of the consciences of Christians, especially Christian lay persons. The fundamental principles of that doctrine require a process of mediation, of dialogue with the social sciences, which brings the social thought of the scriptures into dialogue with the dynamics of contemporary social life and culture. It is not a political manifesto and cannot be simply appropriated as the agenda of any political party. At the same time the term 'doctrine' draws attention to the fact that the Christian cannot simply decide that anything goes in terms of social conscience and that certain underlying principles of the social doctrine, especially those closest to the kernel of the Church's doctrine, have binding character in their own right.

In addition to its strong emphasis on the subjectivity of the person, Catholic social doctrine recognises clearly the legitimate autonomy of the secular order and of the human sciences.

> Respect for the legitimate autonomy of earthly realities prompts the Church not to claim specific competence of a technical or temporal order, but this does not prevent her from intervening to show how, in the different choices made by men and women, these values are either affirmed or denied. (197)

Catholic social doctrine respects the autonomy of the secular order but does not abandon its role in social realities. In his encyclical *Deus caritas est* Pope Benedict XVI notes that 'The Church's social doctrine argues on the basis of reason and natural law, namely on the basis of what is in accord with the nature of every human being' (28 a). The encyclical also notes here that:

> ... it is not the Church's responsibility to make this doctrine prevail in political life. Rather the Church wishes to help form consciences in political life and to stimulate greater insight into authentic requirements of justice as well and greater readiness to act accordingly, even when this might involve conflict with situations of personal interest.

Pope Benedict assigns a very strong role and responsibility precisely to politics in the creation of a just society.

The encyclical notes that building a just social and civil order is a task which must be taken up anew by every generation. The Irish Church needs a more active, articulate laity. We need more lay persons who understand and assume their responsibilities as Christian believers in various aspects of society, inspired by the Social Doctrine of the Church. Pope Benedict's encyclical stresses that 'the direct duty to work for a just ordering of society is proper to the lay faithful' (29). Irish society would benefit from a new generation of lay persons well prepared and capable of informing scientific research, culture and public opinion and political life on how the message of Jesus can be applied to social realities in the pluralistic Irish political and social context. Every generation must take up anew the application of the social doctrine of the Church. A modern knowledge-based economy, for example, is something different to the more static industrial economy of earlier years. The social teaching must address economic realities as they exist, rather than supporting or shooting down some model which is no longer realistically there.

In his encyclical *Centesimus annus* Pope John Paul II set out to address the challenge facing the European former communist countries of moving from centralised economies to a modern market-driven economy. This permitted the pope to reflect on the nature of the market. It was often said, for example, that Catholic social doctrine shied away from addressing the question of the free market and especially of profit. The treatment of the market by Pope John Paul II in *Centesimus annus* is differentiated. He stressed the importance of the market, but also its limits, especially in addressing basic human needs. He notes that 'the free market is the most effective instrument for utilizing resources and responding to needs. But this is true only for those needs ... and resources which are marketable' (34). The pope recalls that 'there are collective and qualitative needs which cannot be satisfied by market mechanisms. There are important human needs which escape the market's logic. There are goods which by their very nature cannot and must not be bought or sold' (40). The pope notes 'there is a strict duty of justice and truth not to allow fundamental human needs to remain unsatisfied and not to allow those who are burdened by such needs to perish' (34).

He indicates a fault line which exists in the interaction between economic policy and social policy. This fault line between the economic and the social has to be addressed by politics. Economic growth is needed to reduce poverty and provide better social services. But economic growth on its own will not redress poverty, disadvantage and gross inequalities. There is need today for a clear political vision – based on sound economic policies, but political in its essence – of how to approach disadvantage. Irish people are proud to be told that their economic model is an example to other countries and that all our economic indicators are on the higher levels of all the comparative charts. But they also want to see their social indicators correspondingly high on the charts. Economic success which is not accompanied by quality health and social services and by quality education for all will leave voters unhappy. Certainly efficiency in the use of resources is important. But education and health care belong to those 'qualitative goods' which cannot be bought or sold or managed simply on the principles of market logic. These services must be marked by 'excellence' and 'quality', measured by human standards. The market must always be accompanied by a strong ethical and juridical framework. As a bottom line an ethical framework is needed for the economy to function. It is needed also in order to place the market at the service of human freedom in its totality. In a world dominated by economic and utilitarian values we have always to recall the words of Pope John Paul in *Centesimus annus*: 'The economy is only one aspect and one dimension of the whole of human activity.' (39)

The fundamental principle of any policy on social advancement is therefore that of *enhancing human capacity*. People are not the objects of social policy. They are its subjects. Subjectivity is of the essence to being human. Every individual is created with unique dignity, created in God's image, male and female. Human beings, in whatever their social situation, are subjects with potential. The more individuals are enabled to realise that potential the better it will be for all. This is why the social doctrine of the Church advocates the principle of inclusion as a fundamental principle for its action. That means that persons living in poverty or in situations of disadvantage must be looked on as brothers or sisters, having the same dignity and the same fundamental rights as I have. They want to be able to place their human talents at the service of their own future and that of their families. Above all they want voice. They want to be the subjects of their own future and that of their communities. This applies both within an individual nation, within our continent and on a global level. Globalisation will be worthy of its name only if it enhances the unity of the human family. Any form of globalisation which breeds exclusion, marginalisation and gross inequality does not have the right to call itself global. Globalisation has to be made the synonym of inclusiveness. An international community must be consistent in realising its commitments. Promises that are made regarding international development are promises made to the poor. Failure to keep one's word is failing the poor. This means placing the human person at the centre of its concerns in the economic sphere. Again here we see the differentiated approach of Pope John Paul II. He recognises the basic nature of the modern business enterprise and the centrality of profit to such enterprise. He notes that when a firm makes a profit, it means that productive factors have been properly employed. Inefficient use of resources is a form of moral irresponsibility. Inefficient use of public funds and resources is very often just another form of corruption. And as always the first victims of corruption are the poor. But again the pope stresses that profitability is not the only indicator of the condition of a business enterprise (cf. *Centesimus annus*, 34). 'It is possible,' the pope says, 'for the financial accounts to be in order, and yet for the people – who make up the firm's most valuable asset – to be humiliated and their dignity offended.' The business enterprise, according to the pope, is above all a community of persons. He stresses that where the conditions of that community are not good, this can actually have negative repercussions on a firm's economic efficiency.

When I first read those paragraphs, I felt that perhaps it was easy to apply these to a small family enterprise where everyone knows everyone else. But what of a huge, modern, multinational enterprise or even a smaller local enterprise where the workers may be scattered around the world working on various levels of subcontract? But then I realised that we have to apply these fundamental principles also to the realities of today. We cannot say that because I do not know my workers directly, as in the old family business, I no longer have responsibility concerning them. Conscience and social responsibility cannot be outsourced. To make this possible we need new forms of international cooperation to provide realistic but robust norms for worker protection. The International Labour Organisation has how this is possible. It is much more difficult to situate this question in ongoing trade negotiations. Public opinion is also important here. When consumers begin to tell us that they are not just concerned with the designer label on their sports shirt, but also the labour conditions within which it was made, then the business community will respond more rapidly. Public opinion and especially consumer opinion can have an important effect on globalisation and on the place we want to see assigned in the process to people and to the environment. The social teaching of the Church must bring its contribution to the process of educating and enlightening public opinion.

Let me come back from global realities to our own island of Ireland. What does it mean in Ireland today to talk about 'a shared humanism based on solidarity'. A particular challenge that we in Ireland have to face is how to foster a new vision of inclusion on our own island. I am referring to North–South relations and the future place of the various religious and cultural traditions in Ireland, no matter what the particular political context. Irish politics has tended at times to look at the 'national question' and the 'economic question' as separate. The nature of a modern economy will inevitably bring home to us the fact that the future of the Irish economy will depend on the integration of all on this island into a functioning, albeit complex, economic unit. To do this we will have to move from a culture built on misunderstanding and exclusion to one of solidarity and inclusion. In its turn this will require a new culture of sensitivity to the way in which different groups in our society understand themselves. There is no way in which we in the South can treat the situation in Northern Ireland as if it did not concern us. An all-Ireland economy would benefit through the revitalisation of the traditional industrial heritage of the North. But our concern should not appear as some kind of subterfuge take-over attempt from Dublin. Economic unity does not require the abandonment of particular identities as the European experience has shown us.

The fact of economic interdependence, especially within the framework of the European Union and the growing multicultural reality of the island, inevitably means that the notion of being Irish will change. We have to work to ensure that people who come from beyond our shores to seek a better life and who contribute to our economic and social development are treated with dignity and are welcomed to become protagonists of a common future. It would be sad if at the same time Irish people of different cultural or religious backgrounds felt that they were less appreciated and welcomed or that they could not maintain their own cultural identity.

Violence, intimidation, hatred and exclusion are not the signs of a mature political culture. Catholic social doctrine, according to Pope Benedict XVI, must become 'a set of fundamental guidelines that are valid beyond the confines of the Church' (27). It must strive to become a shared humanism based on solidarity, drawing also from the various Christian denominations who belong to our Ireland and with whom we share the same citizenry on an equal footing. The challenges of secularism make the fact of religious divides on our island all the more scandalous and frustrating. We need to move forward to seek new ways of working together, of understanding difference and of rejoicing in it. The political process must be accompanied by a more active community process, in which communities work together, not afraid of setbacks along the road.

The social teaching of the Church has to be tested on the ground. The principles are there. We need people to take up the challenge in a wide range of areas, in different contexts. One of my mentors, Cardinal Roger Etchegaray, always said that after the publication of a social encyclical the writing of the next encyclical begins the following day, not on the desk of the pope, but in the lives of active Christian lay men and women who begin testing the teaching in the realities of the world in which they live.

8

SOLIDARITY AND FREEDOM: Defending the Rights and Dignity of Work in a Global Economy

David Begg

One Monday morning a few weeks ago I was passing through Merchant's Arch on my way to a meeting. There was a woman lying on the cobblestones, apparently unconscious. I guessed she was in her mid-thirties. Was she ill or just 'stoned'? What to do in such circumstances poses a real dilemma. If you were to stop for every person in similar circumstances that you come across you'd have a full-time job. But this woman looked ill all the same. I resolved my dilemma by asking the porter in the Central Bank to call an ambulance for her. When I made my return journey she was gone – hopefully to be checked out in St James's Hospital.

I am acutely conscious that a genuine Christian, following the example of the Good Samaritan, should have taken a more interventionist course. But what should the Good Samaritan do if he travels the same route every day for several years and finds another victim of the muggers each week at the roadside? Treat each victim with the same kindness? Give up his acts of compassion on the grounds that his purse will not bear the demands? Or begin to ask what is wrong with this particular road or the society through which it passes? Will he begin to suspect that the innkeeper is in league with the muggers? By his rescue efforts is he creating a market for this type of crime?

And why will the authorities not do something about this problem? Why will they not police the road? Perhaps they don't have the resources? Maybe public spending is being curtailed because of overseas military commitments by the Roman army. Perhaps the local business community are objecting to paying rates or corporate taxes. Maybe the innkeeper is an influential member of the local Chamber of Commerce. Perhaps it is that the police trade union is in dispute about overtime and is working to rule?

Luke, Chapter 10, does not consider these angles so it is a good thing to have a *Compendium of the Social Doctrine of the Church* to interpret gospel values in the context of the modern world. Catholic social teaching is rarely mentioned in Ireland today. It has been said of it that it is the Church's best kept secret. One morning on BBC Radio 4 I heard the author Paul Vallely being interviewed about a book he had written entitled *The New Politics – Catholic Social Teaching for the Twenty-First Century*. At the time Tony Blair was promoting the concept of 'The Third Way'. Vallely suggested that if Blair really wanted to find a third way he should talk to his wife. When asked to explain, Vallely pointed out that, as a Catholic, Cherie Blair would know about Catholic social teaching and its focus on 'The Common Good' as a via media between capital and labour which eschews Marxist/Leninist concepts of class war. As a matter of fact the Catholic bishops of England and Wales arguably played some part in the election of the Labour government in 1997 when they published a pastoral entitled *The Common Good* which was widely interpreted as an attack on the Tories. Mr Blair, alas, did not consult his wife and little is heard from him today about a 'third way'. It has been said of him, and it seems to be true, that he is a man who holds opinions strongly – while he holds them! [Since the writing of this article, Tony Blair has been replaced by Gordon Brown as Prime Minister of the United Kingdom.]

In the *Compendium* there are 103 separate references to 'The Common Good'. In fairness this is not a concept over which the Catholic Church has a monopoly. Noam Chomsky, the left-wing American author who attracted a huge following during a recent visit here, wrote a book with that title in 1998.

Let me quote you some extracts from it:

> The goal is a society in which the basic social unit is you and your television set. If the kid next door is hungry, it's not your problem. If the retired couple next door invested their assets badly and are now starving, that's not your problem.
>
> Boards of directors are allowed to work together, so are banks and investors and corporations in alliances with one another and with powerful states. That's just fine. It's just the poor who aren't supposed to cooperate.
>
> Now that ... workers are superfluous, what do you do with them? First of all, you have to make sure they don't notice that society is unfair and try to change that, and the best way to distract them is to get them to hate and fear one another.
>
> ... the power of business propaganda in the US ... has succeeded, to an unusual extent, in breaking down the relations among people and their sense of support for one another.

The *Compendium* takes a more restrained view of the relations between labour and capital but one which is no less powerful when it states :

> The relationship between labour and capital often shows traits of antagonism that take on new forms with the changing of social and economic contexts. In the past, the origin of the conflict between capital and labour was found above all in the fact that the workers put their powers at the disposal of the entrepreneurs, and these, following the principle of maximum profit, tried to establish the lowest possible wages for the work done by the employees. In our present day, this conflict shows

> aspects that are new and perhaps more disquieting: scientific and technological progress and the globalisation of markets, of themselves a source of development and progress, expose workers to the risk of being exploited by the mechanisms of the economy and by the unrestrained quest for productivity. (279)

You might ask what practical evidence is there of this risk exposure of workers. Well, even in our own buoyant economy in which one bank can make a profit of €1.7billion, there are pressures created by the migration of industry to low-cost locations, as evidenced by the closure of NEC in Ballivor with the loss of three hundred and fifty jobs. In tandem with this there is inward migration of people who are vulnerable to exploitation as evidenced by the Irish Ferries and GAMA cases and the capacity of employers to use people in this situation to undermine established rates of pay and conditions in the different sectors of the economy. We have seen in recent years, and despite minimum wage provisions, the emergence of the phenomenon of 'The Working Poor'. Statistically, 19 per cent of our population are deemed to be at risk of poverty.

Yet it is true that Ireland has also benefited from globalisation through foreign direct investment. Part of the difficulty of current public discourse is that protagonists for or against globalisation often do not acknowledge the existence of these separate truths. The challenge is to find a way to deal with this situation, not to deny the reality of it. I will return to this point later.

In 'The New Industrial Society' John Kenneth Galbraith coined the phrase 'Private Affluence and Public Squalor' as a commentary on the type of society America was becoming. Forty years later, in 1999, the UNDP [United Nations Development Programme] asked him to consider how the world had evolved in the intervening period. In essence he said that things had got worse but the main difference was that greed was now held to be a legitimate motivator of behaviour. But has the world really become a more bitterly divided planet?

At one level there has been significant progress. The Cold War, with all its oppression of freedom and proxy wars, is over. More countries are functioning democracies today than at any time in the past. India and China have awoken and their economic progress has the potential to lift millions out of poverty and destitution. Africa, on the other hand, remains what Tony Blair described as a 'blight on the face of civilisation'. To his great credit he has, with Gordon Brown, tried to lead a campaign to bring that tragic continent into the world economy. But the situation for its 750 million people is profoundly depressing.

Some thirty-six of the fifty countries in Africa are currently affected by or on the brink of drought. According to the World Food Programme, 43 million people are experiencing severe food shortages. The problem is exacerbated by incredibly high levels of HIV/AIDS which is killing off a generation of agriculturalists at well as teachers and other key professionals. In many cases structural adjustment programmes imposed by the West have weakened African states' ability to cope. These same programmes have forced cuts in public spending and entrenched the culture of corruption which is so debilitating to the institutional capacity of African countries. War and other forms of conflict cause millions to become refugees or 'internally displaced persons'. Some progress has been made on debt relief and trade liberalisation. Nevertheless, the poorer a country is, the less varied its economy is and the less well equipped it is to counteract the efforts of drought and other climate challenges.

Africa presents us with a unique moral dilemma. Even the best countries like Ethiopia, Uganda, Tanzania and Kenya suffer corruption and human rights abuses. The Church has taken a strong role in advocating for increased aid for Africa, particularly the UN target of .7 per cent of GNP ODA level. Even at .45 per cent of GNP Ireland spends in excess of €450m every year. It is significant money and it cannot be most effectively used by financing individual projects. Most opinion in the development community supports direct budgetary support for African governments. There is, however, a risk that such transfers will be corruptly or inappropriately used. Public opinion is not ready to accept this reality. Taking risks in an effort to lift Africa out of destitution is unavoidable and morally defensible. The plight of Africa's people is so terrible that we cannot insulate ourselves from these consequences. The desperate efforts of so many to emigrate to Europe are the most obvious manifestation of those consequences. Fortress Europe is not a viable long-term option.

The range of problems with which all developed countries are trying to grapple may be summarised as follows:

- How to deal with large migration flows
- The failure of liberal democracy to prevent the growth of inequality
- The unique influence of the United States in the world.

Globalisation is a phenomenon which excites either total opposition or zealous advocacy. Hundred of books have been written about it and its opponents include such establishment figures as George Soros and Joseph Stiglitz. Generally it is associated in the public mind with the rise of China as an industrial power and the migration of industry and services to that country and India. It is in fact a more complex process than that. The radical relaxation of anti-trust enforcement by the Regan administration in the 1980s allowed big companies to expand horizontally. Many producers, once they gained control over their markets, began to outsource less profitable operations. Many suppliers of these services became dependent on the big companies because they had few other pathways to the marketplace. The increasing power of a few trade-orientated companies over entire production and supply systems results in a variety of economic and political ills.

In a production system marked by extreme outsourcing, oligopoly does not result in the end of competition so much as the redirection of competition as leading companies capture more power to set supplier against supplier and worker against worker and even country against country. The latter arises in the battle for foreign direct investment and tax competition between countries to secure it. In reality it is not really the Chinese who are destroying western jobs, or even globalisation as such, but rather the radical change in the structure of industry resulting in the power of the world's largest traders and retailers to pit producer against producer and to capture most or all of the gain from the arbitrage.

Anyone who doubts this analysis ought to go and see the film about Wal-Mart [*Wal-Mart: The High Cost of Low Price*] which controls 30 per cent of the US retail market. The current controversy over the acquisition of the European steelmaker Arcelor by Mittal is another manifestation of the same thing. Likewise the mega merger of Proctor and Gamble and Gillette last year. Another example is the power over renewable energy systems of British Petroleum and Royal Dutch Shell.

So how can the interests of ordinary people and workers be protected in a world which is dominated by powerful corporate supply chains and is willing to accept destitution affecting 750 million people, growing inequality in the developed countries and the degradation of employment conditions? It seems impossible. And yet to accept that is to accept that people no longer have any influence over their own destiny. Such a conclusion would, it seems to me, run directly contrary to everything Catholic social teaching stands for.

Human beings are capable of standing up for what is right but often they have to be pushed a long way before they do. Consider the United States today. Union organisation there has been pushed down to about 13 million or 12 per cent of the labour force. Unions are unable, in many cases, to stop employers from resiling from pension and health care provision. The automobile industry is a case in point. From an employers' perspective huge legacy costs make them uncompetitive against start-up operations, like Toyota, which do not have those costs. Logically they try to shed those legacy costs and workers lose pensions and health care.

This is a serious development in a country that has virtually no universal public health or welfare provision. How will the citizens of the United States react to that? For how long will religious fundamentalism and the so-called 'War on Terror' divert their attention from the reality that the kitty is bare as regards the state providing for them? For how long will they accept a combination of tax cuts for the super rich and increased military spending causing even further reductions in social programmes? What will happen when the 'Baby Boomers' retirement clashes with the accumulated \$2.5trillion deficit – what the economist Paul Krugman reckons the tax cuts will cost, assuming President Bush makes them permanent.

I would like to think that ordinary Americans would sweep the Republicans from office and, like Sweden in the thirties, install a new social democratic progressive era of long duration. I don't think it will happen. Why? Because America has moved too far to the right over the past thirty years ever to come back to the values of Roosevelt's New Deal or Johnson's vision of 'The Great Society'.

In 1968, a short time before he was assassinated, Robert Kennedy made a powerful speech at the University of Kansas. In the course of it he said this:

> Even if we act to erase material poverty, there is another great task. It is to confront the poverty of satisfaction – a lack of purpose and dignity – that inflicts us all. Too much and for too long, we seem to have surrendered community excellence and community values in the mere accumulation of material things ... The gross national product does not allow for the health of our children, the quality of their education, or the joy of their play. It does not include the beauty of our poetry or the strength of our marriages; the intelligence of our public debate or the integrity of our public officials. It measures neither our wit nor our courage; neither our wisdom nor our learning; neither our compassion nor

> our devotion to our country; it measures everything, in short, except that which makes life worthwhile.

Who could imagine anyone in the Democratic Party today making a speech like this? The Democrats have never been a Social Democratic party as we would understand it. Nevertheless, they have moved so far from their working-class base as to mean nothing to those people. They fail to understand that it is not just neo-conservatives who care about moral and religious values. One unfortunate consequence of this is the split at the end of last year in the AFL-CIO (the US equivalent of Congress). Andy Steryn of SEIU [Service Employees International Union] led a breakaway group on the grounds that continued political funding of the Democratic Party would achieve nothing for working people and their organisation in trade unions.

America has a unique value system based on the heritage of the Pilgrim Fathers. It places a superior value on property and individualism. Labour rights are considered inferior to market deregulation and collectivism is frowned upon. Europe is different. Deregulation of the labour market – one of the central institutions of a market economy – is a litmus test that shows how far any society allows capitalism to go. There has always been, ever since the Middle Ages, the idea of a just wage, which the Catholic Church supported, and which it continues to support as the *Compendium* makes clear. When Catholic societies embarked on capitalism in the nineteenth century they tried to retain the idea of the just wage for the worker, and with it notions of the just price, the just profit and even the just enterprise. They still do, and it is the reason Christian democratic parties in mainland Europe are as attached as they are to a less raw or stakeholder-orientated capitalism.

What the Americans say instead is that capitalism is opportunity for all and risk for all; if you win that game you get lucky. It is the alternative tradition of Catholic capitalism, social market capitalism, or stakeholder capitalism – call it what you like – that is congenial to my outlook. As the *Compendium* puts it:

> The Church's social doctrine has not failed to insist on the relationship between labour and capital, placing in evidence both the priority of the first over the second as well as their complementarities. Labour has an intrinsic priority over capital. 'This principle directly concerns the process of production: it is an evident truth that emerges from the whole of man's historical experience.'[593] This 'is part of the abiding heritage of the Church's teaching.' [549] (277)

The whole European project was guided by people whose values were rooted in Catholic social teaching. People like Jean Monnet and Jacque Delores particularly had a vision of a Social Europe in which the process of social dialogue between both sides of industry played a major part. Our own Social Partnership is derived from that model and I agree with Senator Martin Manseragh when he said in his *Irish Times* column on 18 February:

> Right-wing critics claim partnership is undemocratic, as if democracy consisted only of parliamentary majority rule, rather than multi-layered participation in public affairs. While nominally Seanad Éireann is composed along corporatist lines, social partnership is much closer to the real thing. It is corporatism as an extra dimension to democracy, rather than as a substitute for it as envisaged by some in the 1930s.

This finds a clear resonance in the *Compendium* – paragraph 307 states:

> Beyond their function of defending and vindicating, unions have the duty of acting as representatives working for 'the proper arrangement of economic life'

> and of educating the social consciences of workers so that they will feel that they have an active role, according to their proper capacities and aptitudes, in the whole task of economic and social development and in the attainment of the universal common good. [617] Unions and other forms of labour associations are to work in cooperation with other social entities and are to take an interest in the management of public matters. Union organisations have the duty to exercise influence in the political arena, making it duly sensitive to labour problems and helping it to work so that workers' rights are respected.

It would, of course, be a mistake to assume that there is unanimity of opinion on this point. Social Partnership has bitter opponents on the left and on the right. It is opposed on the left by Trotskyites and by others who believe in class conflict and see social reformers as simply propping up an unjust free market capitalism. It is opposed on the right by economic liberals who see social dialogue, and indeed trade unions, as an unwarranted interference with free markets. The latter have very strong support from the business press. Within their lights they are both right. Social Europe and the social dialogue process is reformist rather than revolutionary. Equality springs from a belief that democratic societies are entitled to put constraints on markets. An activist state is required to enforce choices made by the community, to promote the primacy of the public realm and to make manifest the reality that the pre-condition for a just society is a narrowing of inequality. This clearly is anathema to the hard left and equally to the liberal right.

Nevertheless, the battle for the heart and soul of Europe does not involve the Trotskyites left. Their influence is too marginal for that. It is between Social Democrats and Liberals. Since the era of Jacque Delores the Liberals have been in the ascendant, to some extent because social democratic opinion has been in retreat for the last twenty years for reasons which I won't go into now. But the defeat of the Constitutional Referendum in France and the Netherlands may have halted the liberal advance. I should say, in passing, that I think the draft constitution, particularly the Charter of Fundamental Rights, is a good document. It is clear, even if it is somewhat paradoxical, that it was rejected because of a resentment of the Bellicose liberal attitudes of the Commission. I for one am glad that it happened, although I hope that in time it will be possible to have the constitution re-entered and considered on its merits.

One encouraging development in recent weeks is the way the European Parliament dealt with the services directive. It is a good thing for democracy to see the Parliament coming centre stage and trying to work out a practical accommodation between economic and social matters. Doing so is completely in keeping with the tenets of Catholic social teaching. As Paul Vallely says in *The New Politics:*

> The political problem of mankind is to combine three things – economic efficiency, social justice and individual liberty – and the modern age has lost the correct balance between the three elements of this political equation.

There is some hope too in the fact that the conservative parties in Sweden, Canada and Britain are moving towards the centre ground. I suspect too that Angela Merkel would not have achieved the level of popularity she has as leader of a Centrist Government had she become a CDU [Christian Democratic Union] Chancellor. Personally though, if I were a citizen of those countries I would continue to wear a clove of garlic, just in case.

Francis Fukuyama in *The End of History and the Last Man* argued that the end of the Cold War represented a victory for capitalism red in tooth and claw. A lot of people are putting a lot of effort into proving this hypothesis but they are wrong and the signs are to be found by those that seek them. Of particular interest in this regard is an article Fukuyama wrote in the *Guardian* in which he appeared to recant much of his earlier opinions. With the new imperialism being resisted in both the Muslim world and Latin America, growing international demands for social justice and ever greater doubts about whether the environmental crisis can be solved within the existing economic system, the pressure for political and social alternatives will increase. The particular form of society created by twentieth-century communist parties failed because it ignored the human person's right to individual freedom and will never be replicated. But the quest for a just society will not be abandoned. The best definition of the just society that I have seen is by the Polish and Jewish sociologist Zygmunt Bauman who said when asked to speak about it:

> What would the just society be like? The only answer I can offer in good conscience is that a 'Just Society' is a society which thinks it is not just enough, which questions the sufficiency of any achieved level of justice and considers justice always to be a step or more ahead. Above all it is a society that reacts angrily to any case of injustice and promptly sets about correcting it.

Europe, built on the heritage of Catholic social doctrine, offers the best possibilities for a just society. The mission of the European Union is no longer to prevent warfare within its territory – such would be unthinkable today – but rather to tame globalisation in the service of mankind. Europe, given the dysfunctional state of America, is quite simply the hope of the world.

Earlier I mentioned the difficulties of all countries in managing migration flows. It is an acute challenge for Europe and Ireland is in the cockpit of that challenge. With the opening of our labour market to the ten new countries of eastern Europe the non-national component of our workforce has risen to 9 per cent in less than eighteen months. Germany took thirty years to get to this point. This poses a unique challenge, in justice, to our society. I want to try to relate it to our discussion today because I think most people will admit that the role of the trade union movement is central in this matter.

During the course of the second Nice Referendum the accession of the ten new members was not expected to produce the numbers of immigrants it did. Congress campaigned strongly in favour of the Nice Referendum. We took the main burden of argument against those who said that the country would be swamped by people coming to take Irish jobs. We do not regret taking that stand but we have to admit that we underestimated the push-pull factors that subsequently attracted people here. The evidence available at the time, based on the empirical experience of the entry of Spain, Portugal and Greece, suggested that migration overall would be small and negligible for Ireland given its peripheral location. What essentially undermined that analysis was a combination of Ireland's decision not to avail of the derogation contained in the Nice Treaty to open up its labour market and the opposite decision by the other twelve countries to do so. We were not alone in forming the judgement we did because the ESRI forecast relatively modest numbers of net immigrants of 5000 in 2004, 14,000 in 2005 and 19,000 in 2006. As we now know, there was net immigration of 53,400 people in the year to April 2005.

This is the position we have taken on the matter in the current talks. We are offering employers and government a bargain. We retain the principle of labour mobility but it must be on our terms. Our terms will require the protection of indigenous and non-Irish nationals alike from exploitation and displacement. The measures we propose will not offend against genuine economic efficiency but they will invoke an equal commitment to social justice. This will require a new legal framework, the allocation of sufficient resources to ensure enforcement and strong enough sanctions to promote a culture of compliance. We have to make a working assumption that, at some time in the future, there will be another Irish Ferries or another GAMA. If we do not now put in place an architecture for regulating our labour market which is robust enough to deal with such an eventuality then we will have failed in our duty both to the immigrant and the indigenous workforce.

I mentioned at the outset that Catholic social teaching is sometimes regarded as the Church's best kept secret. That is true of the times we are in but it wasn't always so. Catholic social teaching attracted advocates in the 1930s where motives were probably genuine but they put it at the service of a political ideology which would be abhorrent to most people today. Prominent academics like James Hogan of UCC and Michael Tierney of UCD made common cause with reactionary intellectual priests like Fr Edward Cahill and Fr Edward Coyne to promote a sort of corporatism as an alternative to democracy rather than enhancement of it. The Blueshirts were the political manifestation of that stream of thought. It must be acknowledged, however, that some Catholic figures, like Fr Flanagan, stood out against this thinking and, indeed, a Christian Brother from Derry actually died fighting for the Republican side in the Spanish Civil War. As you know, mainstream Catholic opinion supported Franco and the Blueshirts who fought – or at least went to Spain ostensibly to fight – on his side.

In the 1950s and 1960s, the Jesuits, to their credit, gave Catholic social teaching a new impetus. Many generations of trade union activists participated in adult education programmes through the Catholic Workers' College, later the College on Industrial Relations. Nevertheless, from the 1930s through to the 1960s the Church was a cold place for people with left-leaning sympathies. In part this was shaped by an anti-Communist paranoia characteristic of the Cold War period. It has been said of that period that if four members of a left wing group held a meeting, one would be a representative of the CIA, one would be Special Branch and two would be looking out for the interests of John Charles McQuaid.

The emergence of Catholic policy in Ireland post-independence was unusual in a European context. Many European countries developed along separate confessional lives most notably, for example, in the trade union movement. Many European countries have separate Catholic, Protestant and secular socialist trade union centres. The same pattern emerged in politics. That didn't happen in Ireland because it was assumed that everybody more or less subscribed to a Catholic orthodoxy.

On the whole this was not, I think, healthy, although as a child of the 1950s I have no sense of the oppressive society that one would judge it to have been in retrospect. Yet it cannot be denied that any significant social legislation from the equal pay directives of the 1970s on came from Europe and was, in many cases, resisted by legislators here. The irony of this is that, as I have argued earlier, the European Social Market construct is based on Catholic social values. So my thesis is that the Irish Church has made many mistakes in the last eighty years. Its authoritarianism has damaged it and concealed from full public evaluation the richness of its social teaching. But things are different now. Many Church organisations are strong advocates of social justice. People like Fr Sean Healy and Sr Bridget Reynolds have been to the forefront of public debate about social and economic policy. Trócaire is a strong advocate for justice in relation to our policy towards the developing world.

I am surprised that Noam Chomsky attracted such an enormous following when he came here. He is one of the most powerful intellects in the world today but I doubt that all these people who attended his lectures occupy the same political space that he does. What this confirms in my own mind is that people, while displaying all the attributes of individualism and consumerism, still feel uneasy about the enormous growth of corporate power in a globalised world on the one hand, and the diminution of social solidarity on the other. They have no reference point against which to critically evaluate these trends. In short they no longer have a value system.

This is the challenge for the Church in the modern world. It has to transcend its own recent humiliation and the preoccupation with defining morality only in terms of sexual morals – which, let's face it, it can no longer credibly do anyway. Catholic social teaching, as presented in this *Compendium*, is not about that. It is about a code of Christian ethics and values designed to promote the common good. People of faith and people of no religious conviction but who care about the common good will see it as timely and engage with it. It should cease to be the Church's best kept secret!

Lord [Chris] Patten, in his recent book *Not Quite a Diplomat*, seems to take a sceptical view of Catholic social teaching:

> The identification of the EU with the Catholic Church and Catholic political and social teaching has always made it a harder sell in Britain than it might otherwise have been.

And again:

> Catholic social policy has always caused anxiety, mixing (as it often does) wafflingly well meaning and incompatible aims with a dirigiste instinct increasingly out of sympathy with the times.

From what I have said so far you will not be surprised when I say that I take a more benign view. I am a Social Democrat and Mr Patten is a Conservative, and British Conservatives have not much empathy with even mainland European Christian Democrats, even if Mr Cameron is moving his party towards the centre ground. Then again the centre ground in Britain is defined by Mr Blair who has not much regard for European Social Democrats. So we are at odds. But let me qualify my point by saying that I consider the best manifestation of Catholic social teaching – as represented by the political equation embracing economic efficiency, individual freedom and social justice – to be found in the Nordic countries. The Nordic countries are always in the top ten for competitiveness, productivity and social cohesion. The Nordic countries have high levels of public services supported by high levels of taxation. They are the direct antithesis of the Anglo Saxon model that European liberals want us to adopt. The only complication in this is that the Nordic countries are in the Lutheran tradition!

Pope Benedict's first encyclical makes it clear that there is no room in the community of believers for a poverty that denies anything essential for a dignified life ... the concept of neighbour is universalised.

There is a great film about the life and times of Johnny Cash. One of Johnny's best albums was recorded in Folsom Prison. He was a man who had a sense of what it meant to love your neighbour. When he asked his record company to make the recording they didn't want to do it. There is a scene in the film where the man in charge of the record company says to him: 'Look John, your fans are all Christians. They won't want to see you giving comfort to a gang of rapists and murderers.' To which Johnny replies: 'Well they ain't Christians then.'

I started off by explaining why I thought the parable of the Good Samaritan needed to be interpreted for the modern world. However, Matthew 25:31-46 is direct and more explicit:

> I was hungry and you never gave me food; I was thirsty and you never gave me anything to drink; I was a stranger and you never made me welcome; naked and you never clothed me; sick and in prison and you never visited me.

It does not, it seems to me, require much intellectual effort to see how this powerful injunction applies to our times. The Good Samaritan acts immediately and without qualification to relieve the urgent physical suffering of another person. Remember too that the Good Samaritan is a foreigner!

9

MORALITY AND THE MARKET: The *Compendium* on the Economy

Ray Kinsella

The *Compendium* is a landmark contribution to our understanding of the root causes of global imbalances in wealth and political power as well as exploitation-driven environmental degradation. It sets out the consequences of these realities, in particular for the individual person and for the family. These are, the *Compendium* argues, the cornerstones of society; they should, therefore, be free from subjugation in any form, by the state and/or corporate sectors. More positively, the *Compendium* sets out a values and principles-based framework, within which *sustainable* global development can be achieved.

The *Compendium* is, at one level, a rigorous synthesis of the social teaching of the Catholic Church. These teachings embrace the whole social, economic and scientific order. The *Compendium* draws on the great papal encyclicals, notably in the period since Leo XIII's *Rerum Novarum*. It is also informed by a wide range of addresses, by successive popes, to specialised audiences and, also, of ongoing dialogue with them. The unique philosophical insight of Pope John Paul II – focused on the innate dignity of the human person – permeates the whole analysis. The roots of the synthesis, however, go deeper. They encompass, and build on, the whole Judaeo-Christian tradition.

At another level, the *Compendium* is timely, to the point of being prophetic. It addresses the nihilism which is at the heart of much of western mainstream thinking on the human Person, especially within the context of work, and which has infected market-based economic and political systems.

Most importantly of all, the *Compendium* provides an alternative values-based vision of the future of the new *globalised* economic and environmental paradigm. It sets out the case that a sustainable politico-economic system – or, at the micro-level, 'Business Model' – can only be built on a set of 'universal' values.

At the heart of this perspective is the transcendent value of the individual human person. This reality, by definition, requires a decision-making process, based on values, which are aligned to the dignity of the person. These values apply equally to the employee and the employer, to the small company and to the internationally mobile multinational company, operating in the developed world as well as in vulnerable, indebted developing countries.

The *Compendium* is not prescriptive in regard to specific 'Business Models' or organisational systems. But it is emphatic that any such models or systems must, in their mind-set and operation, be values-based, in their regard to their interaction, in whatever form, with the human person.[1]

Crisis in western markets-based corporatism

This contribution is focused on the narrower issue of the *Compendium*'s analysis of markets and morality. The connection between the two is key to its wider analysis. This is for two reasons. The first is this. The fall of Soviet Communism, with its Statist economy, in the late 1980s and the more recent development of Communist China's *economy* have contributed to the pre-eminence of the western free-markets-based paradigm. There is compelling evidence that this system is in crises.

The symptoms are many. They range from the nihilism of western consumerism through to a total asymmetry in political power, uninformed by any understanding of substantive principles identified in the *Compendium* such as 'common good' or 'social solidarity'. The system is in crisis precisely because it has become detached from any *lived* experience of morality and order.

It is important to be clear about what is meant by 'order'. The final end of the person is to be open to the love of God. It follows that the different domains within which they work out and affirm this end on earth must be so *ordered* as to facilitate its achievement. This requires, in practice, respect within the workplace. It means corporate leadership, characterised by humility. It means that the wealth produced within economics is intended not just to meet the needs of the privileged few but, rather, that there is a 'universal' destination of wealth, which takes precedence. This must be reflected in the ethos of the company as well as in national and international laws and governance.

The near-global financial crises of the late 1980s – notably the Asian Banking 'contagion' and the near-implosion of the Hedge Fund Long Term Capital Management (LTCM) – provided a glimpse of the consequences of ignoring, or 'crowding out', these values and principles. The corporate failures of the mid-1990s to the early 2000s – for which Enron now stands as a metaphor – disclosed, notably in the US but not only there, a *moral* malaise that generated enormous human as well as economic costs.

The ascendancy of the short-term Shareholder Value Maximisation 'Business Model' infected the market-based economy and 'crowded out' any acknowledgement of the dignity of the person. Market information was distorted, and corporate balance sheets manipulated in order to inflate earnings and, therefore, the market-based value of the company. It would be more accurate to say that the concept of 'person' simply did not exist within this construct. Individuals were 'resources'; they were commodities to be used, exploited, coerced, bullied – and disposed of – without any regard to their *innate* dignity and their final end. This was serious disorder.

Within western mainstream markets, formerly 'high trust' market institutions were drawn into an ethical 'Black Hole'. These ranged from banks through institutional investors, as well as accountancy firms and auditors who had quasi-guardianship of the markets-based model and on whose integrity the whole corporate-markets axis rested.[2] Not all, by any means – moreover the overwhelming majority of individuals working in these institutions were undoubtedly highly moral.[3] But there were enough to subvert morality and order within the markets and to denigrate the intrinsic value of the person. The consequences of this disorder, stemming from the lack of any values- or principles-based system of governance or management, were visited on employees of wealth-fixated corporates, on small investors misled by false information, on pensioners and most evidently on senior management of these companies, seduced by the lie on which the 'Business Model' was based.

Major companies were destroyed, tens of thousands of jobs lost, fines of hundreds of millions of dollars were imposed by the US regulatory authorities on swathes of institutions; executives in manacles, families shredded – this was all a part of the 'collateral damage' caused by the absence of morality within a 'Business Model' that subverted the role of markets.

Against this backdrop, the case for a values-based system, focused on the dignity of the person and the unique role of the family, is less an aspiration and more an imperative for markets to be able to function at all, let alone fulfil their role in terms of economic efficiency.

The dominant mind-set –'greed is good'[4] – had this effect: the values by which individual persons attempt to order their lives behind their hall doors were increasingly (and violently) put at odds with the 'values' that drove corporate activity behind their office door.

The emptiness, the lie, should have been evident from the 'coffee time' chatter and clichés: 'Move up or Move out'; 'If you can't turn up on Saturday, don't bother coming in on Sunday'; 'Least Value Employee (LVE)'. It was, of course, nonsense, except for those persons caught up in such nightmares. The point is that it shaped the corporate environment. It devalued and 'commoditised' the person and was intensely destructive of relationships – especially of the Family – within the wider society, underpinned by the economy. It was doomed commercially, precisely because it was unethical and immoral. Being unethical, it systematically undermined the operation of the market-based economic system; not least, incidentally, in the regulatory overkill (notably the Sarbannes Oxley Act in the US, a classic example of 'regulatory imperialism') that ensued.

Trust is what individuals (and, it is no coincidence, banking institutions) seek out most in any relationship. Trust is imperative for the functioning of markets. Trust was the first casualty of the mainstream adoption of 'Business Models' that were/are obsessed, above all else, with maximising wealth for privileged elites within the corporate sector.

This takes us back to the paradox noted above; on the one hand, the near contemporaneous triumph of the western market-based economic systems and, on the other hand, the deep crises in this same system. It is within this space that the *Compendium* makes its prophetic case for change.

In the wake of the corporate crises, governments have of course legislated for reforms to financial regulation, strengthened accounting and auditing standards as well as implemented changes in corporate governance. They have, incidentally, done so without seeing the 'beam' in their own eye.

Reforms are a necessary, but not a sufficient, response to the emergence of systemic crises, slowly gathering momentum across three fronts: global poverty, in particular the AIDS pandemic; corporate nihilism in the wealth-fixated market-based western 'democracies'; and an unprecedented threat to the global environment, which is largely induced by the excesses of these latter countries.

In terms of responding to these threats, the *Compendium* upholds the dignity of the person and, by extension, of the family, as well as their respective responsibilities. Any real understanding of the nature of these threats – in other words, just what is being threatened – starts from the effects of a denial of the fundamental freedoms of the person, which finds its potential for realising the dignity with which it was created, within the family. So, too, does a response to these same threats.

The *Compendium* deals in 'universals', which are simply realities that can be instinctively understood and acted upon as being 'good' and 'right' by all persons open to truth. It steadfastly avoids criticism of individual countries and/or regimes. Instead, it sets out the fundamental values and principles by which such countries – and we, as individuals – stand condemned and challenged.

A perspective on markets

Economic agents – from the small farmer to the multinational corporate – operate within an extraordinary range of economic systems, social constraints (e.g. social partnership) and 'Business Models'. The products and services generated by economic agents are, for the most part, traded through markets. These 'markets' range from the informal stalls on which farmers in less developed countries sell vegetables or crafts, through to high octane, IT-based, 24/7 global financial markets.

Organised markets are the central nervous systems of national economies, as well as of the increasingly open and interdependent global economy. They generate significant benefits or, more formally, 'welfare gains' to the individual, the family and the wider community which is underpinned by economies functioning through markets of different kinds. These benefits arise primarily because markets reduce the costs of acquiring the information necessary to allow producers (savers) and purchasers (investors) to meet on common ground. Note the absolutely central role of information, and, by extension, the importance of the integrity and timeliness of such information. This information allows markets to generate (relative) prices based on the demand for, and the supply of, assets. Such assets range from goods and services which are directly consumed at the point of production, through to tradable services and on to highly complex financial assets, which have less to do with production and are more related to managing/transferring risk, speculation and arbitrage.

In other words, markets are based on information. Equally, efficient markets generate information that would otherwise be impossible or highly costly to produce. Importantly, just as the existence of markets are predicated on certain human freedoms, the operation of markets requires honesty, transparency and 'fair dealing', in order to encourage individuals to participate in such markets. The greater the degree of participation in such markets, the deeper, more liquid and, therefore, efficient are markets.

Conversely, an erosion of trust regarding information arising from a lack of honesty, integrity or transparency will fracture markets, leading to the possibility of default and the impossibility – except at a wholly disproportionate cost – of enforcing market contracts.

Markets incentivise the production of goods and services. More specifically, they incentivise the production of a *surplus* for exchange trade. This enhances the welfare of the individual and of the wider community of which they are a part – most immediately, the family.

This surplus can also, as noted, underpin an emergent form of 'contracts', based on specific *underlying* assets. These contracts, called derivatives, are a feature of modern, highly monetised economies. The contract itself is, effectively, separated from the underlying asset. While risk is directly or indirectly embedded in all forms of exchange, derivatives, as the largest category of contacts in financial markets, are now based on the *de facto* 'commoditisation' of risk, only tenuously connected to a underlying asset or e.g. oil, or other sets of assets. The value of trade in such 'derivatives', instruments/contracts is now such that it entirely dominates the value of 'real' transactions. They can also have a powerful impact on the performance and governance of companies, which is quite separate from the real world, work and effort of all those employed in, and by, such companies.

In this regard, the *Compendium* makes an enormously important contribution to contemporary financial market analysis. It notes that:

> The financial sector, which has seen the volume of financial transactions far surpass that of real transactions, runs the risk of developing according to a mentality that has only itself as a point of reference, without being connected to the real foundations of the economy.
>
> A financial economy that is an end unto itself is destined to contradict its goal, since it is no longer in touch with its roots ... it has abandoned its original and essential role of ... contributing to the development of people and the human community. (369)

The point is this. Derivatives have been regarded by the most eminent authorities such as Alan Greenspan (former Chairman of the US Federal Reserve) as being essentially positive. Equally, they have been criticised by market authorities (such as Warren Buffet, the greatest financial entrepreneur and Fund Manager of all time) as 'financial Weapons of Mass Destruction'. This is the point to which markets have evolved. This tests the need for public intervention and regulation, because of the latent threat and possible impact of a global financial crash on people and families and communities, not involved in, but highly vulnerable to, speculation in those esoteric markets.

More generally however, markets have provided the essential dynamic behind the growth of international trade, the rise of political systems and the spread of ideologies. The advent of the internet has given almost unimaginable leverage to markets, broadly defined. A key point made in the preceding sections is that morality – 'right thinking' on exchange, international trade and work are all based on fundamental values – is a necessary condition for the existence and the efficient operation of markets.

Markets are predicated on certain individual freedoms which are based on morality. These include the freedom to work, and to produce, exchange and trade the 'surplus' over and above that required for subsistence. Countries that deny such freedoms lack moral, and therefore political, legitimacy. The denial of such freedoms inhibits economic specialisation and the conditions necessary for international trade and the market systems to operate effectively.

It is important to highlight the point – as the *Compendium* does – that there are important human needs which simply cannot be 'commoditised' and delivered through the market. The most obvious example is the provision of care – medical, educational or emotional – to the poor, dispossessed and marginalised.

The *voluntary* commitment to providing such care, because the human person is, as Sr Consilio, founder of the 'Cuan Mhuire' communities for the care and rehabilitation of victims of addiction, insists, 'made in the image and likeness of God', is an expression of love, which is the core value of the moral order, around which the *Compendium* framework is based.

Subject to this caveat, markets are nonetheless central to the economies which underpin human societies. They embody networking, communication. They generate relative values/prices, which underpin the whole operation of exchange and trade. They empower the individual/family is rooted. Where they are allowed to operate, the positive effects diffuse through the wider communities within which they operate. They create and sustain employment and drive innovation. Markets tell the 'truth', based on *the availability and integrity of information*. They can confound and bring down governments.

This takes us back to the relationship between markets and morality. A 'free act' can be good or bad. 'Bad' means subversive of truth and, therefore, destructive of relationship. Sin, in fact. The capacity to sin is a uniquely human attribute and a measure of the Churches' (and God's) respect for the freedom of the individual person. To put this another way, it is not possible to speak of love (which is at the heart of the *Compendium*'s analysis) if the person is not free to reject love. And the rejection of love is driven by greed and, ultimately, pride. In other words, the primacy of self over the 'other' person.

Case study after case study highlights these all too human deficiencies and their destructive impact on institutions, which go to make up a 'market'. The effective operation of markets – their capacity to generate welfare gains – requires, above all, trust, which is based on Truth. Whatever the extent of (over) regulation, markets will always be vulnerable to manipulation for personal or corporate gain by individuals, corporate, cartels and government. Where this happens, first and second order consequences will be catastrophic. The damage in human terms to the person and to the economic system in which they function is incalculable. In the absence of moral order, markets stall, fracture and even undergo a 'meltdown', until trust is restored.

Markets are, therefore, institutions of the highest social importance. It is no coincidence that they operate most effectively in real democracies (which can ensure basic freedoms) and within a system of governance and regulation that is 'high trust' in nature and characterised by honesty and integrity. Paradoxically, they can, for these very same reasons, be subverted.

This reality highlights two key points made in the *Compendium*. The first is what it calls 'the concrete risk of an idolatry of the market'. Markets are a means to a greater end. The market, as the *Compendium* underlines, 'cannot find in itself the principles of its own legitimisation'. This, the *Compendium* points out, 'belongs to the consciences of individuals and to the role of the state'.

The consequences of a lack of morality in relation to the first point are very clear from a critique of corporate debacles in recent years, which aimed at manipulating the market. In relation to the second point, the role of the state, the key point is that, notwithstanding the central economic and societal role of the market, there are limits to the scope of markets. At the limit, it is the role of the state to decide on an appropriate framework for the oversight and regulation of markets. This does not dilute the responsibility of institutions or individuals for ensuring the integrity of market transactions.

Deconstruction of the *Compendium*[5]

It is important to understand the 'scaffolding' on which the *Compendium* rests. This, in turn, demonstrates both its rigour and manner in which it integrates a *person*-centred vision of the economy, operating within free competitive markets with an ethically based system of global economic and political governance.

Figure 1 (p. 167) provides a schematic 'deconstruction' of the *Compendium*. It attempts to distil the key elements of the *Compendium*, the values on which it rests and the normative principles which it generates. These apply across all peoples and cultures because they are aligned to the natural law. They resonate with the prescriptive teachings and the insights of the Torah and Talmud, the Old and especially New Testament and, also, the Qur'an; the emphasis differs, but at the heart of each is the transcendent dignity of the person and the application of the 'golden rule', across all domains of human existence, including economics and markets.

Figure 1 highlights a number of points of particular relevance. The first is this. It immediately becomes apparent that the analysis of the *Compendium* is based on values. We are therefore into the realm of the intellect and free will of the individual person. In effect, these values are, in terms of their application, 'universals'. All persons – worker, entrepreneur, policy maker – have an *instinctive* understanding of such values 'hard wired' into their understanding. This understanding can – and has been – subverted and subjugated by ideology, as well as by wealth and is highlighted in one of the *Compendium*'s most striking phrases, 'an "idolatry" of the market'; as if there were not higher values to which both the functioning and outputs of markets are subject (349).

The *Compendium* identifies and validates these values as the indispensable basis of any sustainable market-based system of economics and politics. 'Markets' are, in themselves, 'neutral' with respect to the concept of morality. But – and this is the point – they can only function effectively within a framework based on moral values. This argument admits of no exceptions.

These values, as set out in Figure 1 based on the *Compendium*, are truth, freedom and justice. The *Compendium* develops the scope of each of these values. It is insistent on the relevance of love as the origin of these values. It asserts: 'Love ... must be reconsidered in its authentic value as the highest and universal criterion of the whole of social ethics.'(204) This applies to the manner in which a company is managed in all its aspects. It applies to the strategy of multinational corporates. And it applies to applications of law, regulation and 'best practice' by governments in international trade, which is mediated through markets.

Figure 1 underlines a second important point in this 'deconstruction' which follows on from the first. Values generate principles, by which human actions, behaviour and – in 'business speak' – 'strategy' are directed towards the 'highest and universal criteria'. These principles are the 'common good', 'subsidiary' and 'social solidarity'. The *Compendium* develops this argument at length. It is, however, worth stressing the point that the authority of the *Compendium*'s argument is based upon the life of Jesus Christ, as set out in the New Testament and, equally, in the teaching of the Church, which is His mystical body. This has seldom been more effectively stated than by St Paul, when writing to his fellow Christians in Corinth:

> Remember how generous the Lord Jesus was: he was rich, but he became poor for your sake, to make you rich out of his poverty. This does not mean that to give relief to others you ought to make things difficult for yourselves: it is a question of balancing what happens to be your surplus now against their present need, and one day they may have something to spare that will supply their own need. That is how we strike a balance: as Scripture says: The man who gathered much had none too much, the man who gathered little did not go short. (Cor 8:7-9; 13-15)

The 'Person' in a market-based system

The innate dignity of the individual person is acknowledged, particularly by the great Theistic religions of Judaism, Islam and Christianity.[5] In each of these, the morality of transactions entered into by individuals are explicitly acknowledged. It is the person who enters into these transactions – and individual persons who are impacted by them. Transactions, including those mediated through the markets, are therefore subject to moral norms. The Torah, for example, states that when a Jew meets with God in judgement, the first question they will be asked is whether or not they were honest in their business dealings. Integrity in business relationships, based on *intention* as well as word, is an integral element of both the Jewish and Islamic faiths.

Christianity is predicated on the transcendent Nature of the person and on relationships. This is true on two levels. First, the nature of God as a trinity of *persons* in an infinite, eternal, procession-based *relationship* of love. Second, the incarnation of the second person of the Most Holy Trinity, taking on a fully human nature; being born in historical time of the Virgin Mary, living in relationships, with a world of work, emigration, trade-based markets and finance. The Incarnation reconciled the human person with his Creator, in whose image he is created. By so doing, the individual is restored to relationship based on the right use of free will – as sons and daughters of God in Jesus. Such reconciliation was necessitated by the effects of the wrong use of will by our first parents: a refusal to acknowledge the rights of the Creator, in whom fulfilment and ultimate happiness alone subsists.

In the providence of God, the incarnation was accomplished through the voluntary suffering and death ('like man, in all things, save sin') and resurrection of Jesus. This is the ultimate expression of God's love for the human person and source of the gospel imperative addressed to all persons, in all circumstances: 'Love one another, as I have loved you.' This injunction – which resonates with the *Compendium*'s compelling imperative that 'love must be reconsidered within its authentic value as the highest and universal criterion of the whole world' – encompasses all dimensions of the person. The person lives, and works out their contingent (that is, driven by intellect, free will and responsiveness to grace) relationship with God within the world of work.

In this context, the centrality of the person is always paramount. The *Compendium* points out that: 'The human person is the measure of the dignity of work ... human work has an ethical value of its own which clearly and directly remains linked to the fact that the one who carries it out is a person.' (271) The outcomes of work are, as noted earlier, mediated through mechanisms of exchange, including highly developed global markets in finance and commodities. The Incarnation means that this process is touched by – and directed towards – the Divine. This is the basis of the rigour and logic of the *Compendium*'s analysis, with its interface of values and principles; of love and the human person.

An economic system – a 'Business Model' – that subjugates the person may take the form of totalitarianism in some form or other. Or it can be driven by substituting the outcomes of work – wealth creation/economic surplus – for its final end. Wealth, as an end in itself – or, as is frequently observable in the corporate sector, a surrogate for power over other persons – is wholly at variance with the 'universal criteria' of love. This, in fact, is frequently found to be the main cause of the implosion of a major corporate, since power is the means by which Internal Controls are undermined, instead of being directed towards maintaining the integrity of business process.

The centre of gravity of the 'new economy' is knowledge. At the heart of the global productive process is intellectual capital. Man's intellectual capacity is, largely, what animates his essentially spiritual nature. Wealth, *in isolation from principles which direct its use and distribution*, is inevitably destructive of the human person, whose creative genius is actually the essential source of wealth creation.

It is a fundamental error not to acknowledge that *relationship*, which shapes a persons' final destination, should not permeate the environment, including work, within which this destiny is worked out. This reality has to be relearned and acknowledged. Even in the post-Enron reform environment – with its unquestionably positive emphasis on 'business ethics' and 'corporate social responsibility' – mainstream 'corporate speak' and 'policy speak' remain desensitised to the uniqueness of the human person. The almost infinite capacity of the individual for goodness is suffocated by perceptions of the person as a 'human resource'. Such a perspective opens the door to the *de facto disposability* of the individual and the displacement of relationships by contractual arrangements, which is destructive of social solidarity. The *relationship* of 'I' to 'the Other', having its source and fullest expression in the person of Jesus, is essentially one of 'giving'. Conversely, the 'contractual' (as opposed to relationship-based) model of work is predicated on 'having' (a 'must-have' mindset fixated on the 'I' to the exclusion of all others). That is why the short-term shareholder value maximisation 'Business Model' self-destructed.

The *Compendium*: from the person to the market[7]

Figure 2 (p. 168) follows on from the 'deconstruction' of the values-based model, around which the *Compendium* is built. It is, in effect, the same model, as it operates in the social institutions of market-based economies. The primacy of the person – based on their nature, destiny and, as a consequence, their responsibilities – is at the top of Figure 2.

It is precisely the nature of the person that generates the values and principles by which they are called to live. This, in turn, requires that whatever the political or economic system within which they live and work, the person has certain inalienable rights. These include the right to work and to private property. These rights encompass the value of all work. It means, for example, that unemployment, especially when it is the direct outcome of state and/or corporate policies, is a moral, not just a political issue. This is why the *Compendium* refers to 'the scourge of unemployment'.

This perspective has a pervasive relevance to corporate structures, i.e. the ethos of a company and the principles (or lack of principles) by which it is managed. The *Compendium* is not, in any way, prescriptive regarding these structures. Based on developments in corporate strategy, corporate structures and 'Business Models' are subject to constant, competition-driven change.

The *Compendium* acknowledges and upholds as a necessity the need for profitability. This is an important point. At the same time, it asserts the right of employees to strike and also the legitimate and important role of trade unions. These rights are not absolute; they are bounded. Corporate structures, of whatever kind, can most effectively operate within market-based systems. This has been expanded on earlier and has to do with the role of markets and, also, the fact that there is a powerful synergy between, on the one hand, a values-based sustainable 'Business Model' and, on the other hand, the efficient operation of markets, which requires trust, honesty and transparency.

The *Compendium* notes that there are limits to 'unfettered markets'. It asserts the overriding importance of the 'universal destination' of economic wealth. The Torah (and Talmud) would concur with the *Compendium* that, in principal, wealth is good and profits are imperative. The issue is the *proper use* of wealth. The issue is how profits are generated and how and by what criteria they are distributed. This is where the values and principles, set down at the outset, are of crucial importance. They take precedence over purely market-determined outcomes.

In Figure 2, this iterative process takes us to the economy. At one level, whatever the actual nature of the economy, it will be shaped by the prevailing values, principles and freedoms of society. At a deeper level, the economy – from the Gulag through Wall Street and, by way of contrast, the 'Economy of Community' developed by Chiara Lubich – is an expression of the nature of *community*. Its mode of operation – and public policy management – determine whether or not individuals are free to work out, in relationships (primarily in families), their final destiny to be with God who, as St John in his sublime writings insists, is Love.

But, as noted, the *Compendium* argues that the economy can only be a *partial* answer to the person's innate needs. It is constrained by the 'Universal Destination' of economic wealth. This underpins the intrinsic relationship between morality and economics, including the markets, which are the essential mechanism through which economies function. Getting this balance right is not easy and is subject to constant pressure. Against this background, the *Compendium* makes the point that:

> A business' objective must be met in economic terms and according to economic criteria, but the authentic values that bring about the concrete development of the person and society must not be neglected. (338)

The *Compendium* presses its case further. In doing so, it makes an enormously important contribution to our understanding of the challenges faced by humanity. In Figure 2, this is set out as the 'plateau' of globalisation, analogous to, say, other anthropological 'inflection points' through which humanity has evolved.

The key 'driver' of economic wealth today is not resources or location or even military power. As indicated in Figure 2, in the 'Knowledge Economy',[6] the source and catalyst of what now appears to be an exponential (rather than a 'stepped') process is the intellect – a unique characteristic of the human person.

The key elements of this new stage in the development of humanity and the human person include technology, the emergence of highly mobile multinational companies aligned to the pulse of the global economy, an enormous relative increase in international trade (and, hence, global interdependence). There are, in turn, based on the operation of global, highly innovative sets of these financial markets. This whole new construct has been both generated and brought to the fore by the phenomenon of unprecedented global immigration and the imperative of upholding human rights, not simply inside 'national' jurisdictions but globally. The imperative 'My neighbour is *all* mankind' has taken on a whole new importance.

In these circumstances, the *Compendium* makes a prophetic case for an ethical basis for international arrangements and governance in relation to e.g. economic immigration and, equally, the status of refugees.

The core value is love, the principal is respect for the person, and the rationale is that we are all made in the image and likeness of God, our ultimate goal. This is the *definitive* benchmark for evaluating the morality, not alone of markets but of international regulation and governance across the whole sphere of economic and trade cooperation.

In summary what emerges from a close study of the *Compendium*'s analysis of markets, and the market-based economic system, is this: the outcomes help to explain why corporates (and governments) which do not respect the person frequently self-destruct, with enormous collateral damage to employees and other stakeholders. The evidence suggests that corporates can be highly successful in monetary terms over the shorter term – but that their lack of lived values and principles will, ultimately, bring about their demise.

More positively, it helps to explain why other companies are successful. De Geus, writing in the *Harvard Business Review*, sets out the concept – based on over thirty years' experience of senior management – of the 'Living Company'. His analysis resonates not alone the critique set out in the *Compendium* but also the insights of the Torah and Talmud on work and what is to be valued most in business:

> Why do so many companies die young? ... because their policies and practices are based too heavily on the thinking and language of economics ... because their managers focus exclusively on producing goods and services and forget that the organisation is a community of human beings ... 'Living Companies' know who they are, understand how they fit into the world, value new ideas and new people and husband their money in a way that allows them govern their future.[7]

'Business Models' embedded in ideologies which deny the centrality of the human person – whose defining characteristic is a capacity for an authentic experience of love – will inevitably implode. It is a short step from Red Square, or Tiananmen Square, to Wall Street circa the mid-1990s/early 2000s.

More generally, and in conclusion, there is a striking paradox in the fact that the aftermath of the fall of the Berlin Wall – which stood as a metaphor for a Statist and Godless regime which demeaned and devalued the human person – also saw the rise of the 'greed is good' philosophy and the manner in which it infected mainstream Western, Capitalist thinking and also market practice. The rise of the short-term Shareholder Value Maximisation model led to the manipulation of corporate earnings and balance sheets, leading to the subversion of markets. The consequences were visited on employees of wealth-fixated companies, on small investors and stakeholder of pension funds. Most evidently, it has been visited on senior management investigated and prosecuted by the US regulatory authorities – the SEC and the New York Attorney General, Elliot Spitzer.

Not alone that. Formerly 'high trust' organisations – from banks through institutional investors as well as accountants and auditors – on whose integrity the whole corporate markets axis depends – were drawn into a fundamentally flawed and immoral 'Business Model'.

The overwhelming majority of individuals working in such organisations were undoubtedly highly moral. But the dominant corporate orthodoxy, a 'mindset' of organisations in which they worked, had this effect: the values by which individuals ordered their lives behind their hall doors were at variance with those demanded of them behind their office doors.

Trust is what individuals seek above all in a relationship. Trust is also imperative for the functioning of markets. The interrelationship between morality (which is above all about relationships) and the markets is compelling. Public trust was the inevitable casualty of successive corporate debacles, notably in the US, but also permeating the whole market-based economic and financial system. Regulatory reforms, changes in corporate governance as well as in standards and in oversight of accounting and auditing are a necessary – but not sufficient – response to an ethical crisis in the western, market-based economic system.

The core of the *Compendium* is an interface between Love and the human Person. That is Truth. No dimension – not least work, intermediated through markets and trade – of the human experience is semi-detached from this reality. The *Compendium* sets out a rigorous, evidence-based case that a *sustainable markets-based* economic system can only be built upon a set of values, at the heart of which is the respect for the human person within the family unit.

Figure 1. The Market and the *Compendium:* Values and Principles

Source: Kinsella © 2006

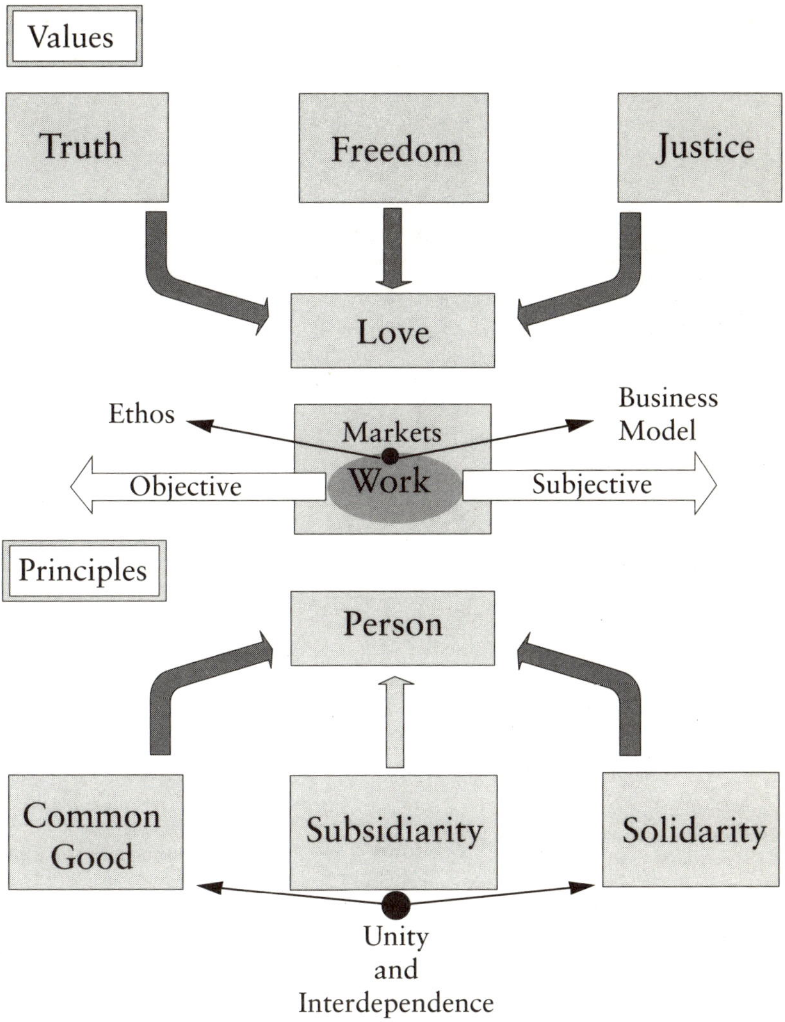

Figure 2. Deconstructing the *Compendium*: The Person, Work and the Global Knowledge-Based Economy Source: Kinsella © 2006

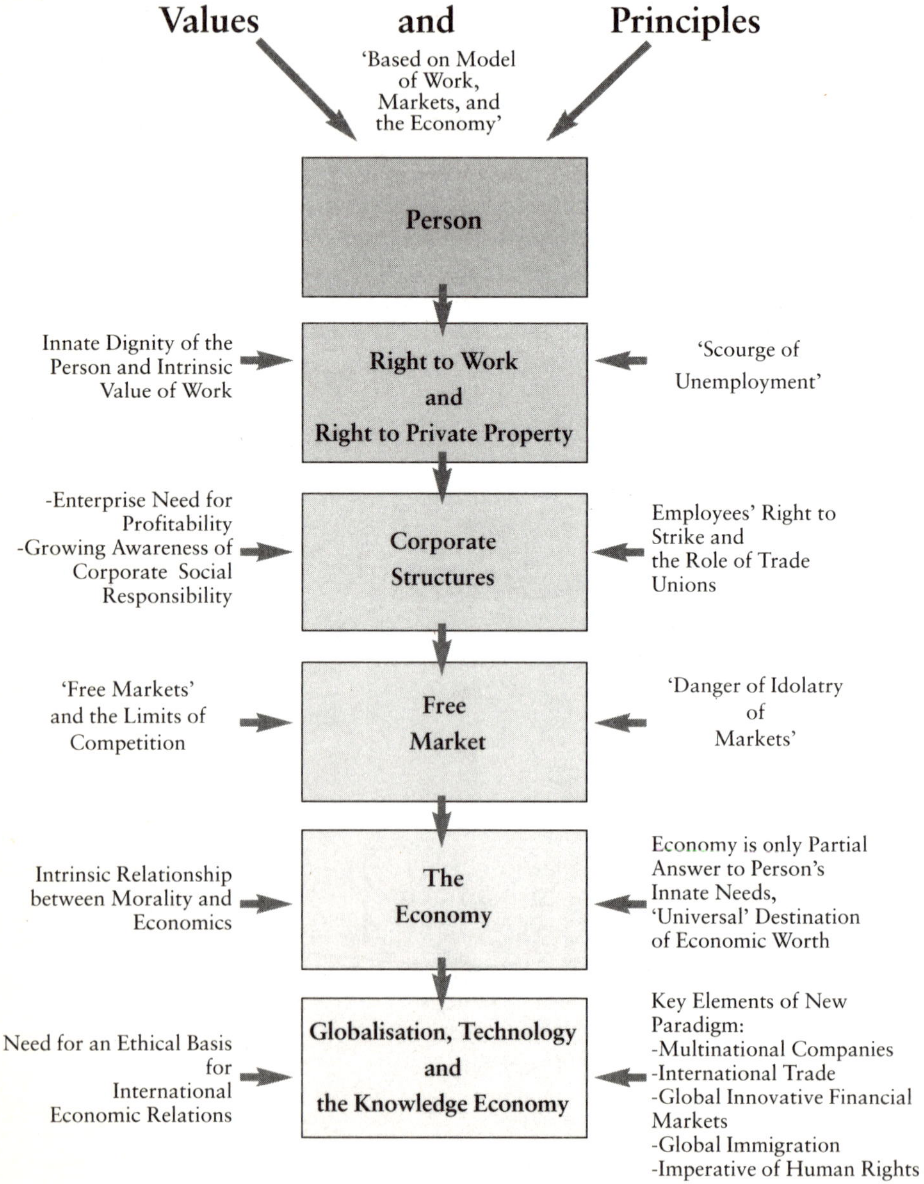

Notes

1 For a complementary treatment of themes covered in this paper, see Kinsella, R. and McNerney, J., 'Corporate Sickness and Corporate Health', *Studies*, 94, p. 376.

2 The 'meltdown' of Anderson's – the global Accountancy and Consultancy firm – was a tragedy for the many thousands of high-calibre, ethical professionals whom it employed.

3 This point was well made by Liam O'Reilly, (then) Chief Executive of the Financial Regulator (Ireland) in his First Report on the AIB Investigation, Irish Financial Services Regulatory Authority [IFSRA], Dublin, 2004.

4 This maxim, from the film *Wall Street*, became a perfect aphorism for a generation – as well as providing an insight into the basic reason for its implosion.

5 It is upheld by other religions and by such great Pagan writers as Marcus Aurelius (see *Meditations*). It is, on the other hand, ultimately rejected by Totalitarianism, in all its forms.

6 See Kinsella R. and McBrierty V., *Ireland and the Knowledge Economy*, Cork, Oak Tree Press, 1998.

7 Arie De Geus, 'The Living Company', *Harvard Business Review*, 1997.

SECTION FOUR

Rights and Responsibilities

10

RIGHTS AND RESPONSIBILITIES: The *Compendium* on Personal Rights and the Common Good

William Binchy

Anyone who is interested in advancing the protection of human rights will be fascinated by the values at the core of the *Compendium*. The *Compendium* is not the same as an international human rights instrument promulgated by international treaty. It does not merely address states and sets out no legal sanctions for non-compliance. It is essentially a philosophical document, undoubtedly written from a religious perspective but equally clearly accessible to all readers who are concerned about human rights.

Human rights are of course normative in character. Contemporary human rights theory[1] can trace its origins to many philosophical and religious sources of inspiration. These sources are by no means agreed as to such basic questions as the nature and purpose of society, the proper remit of law, indeed, the very nature and goals of human life. We therefore find a dynamism and internal debate within human rights theory, which can of course be 'resolved', as a matter of positive law, by the making of some new international treaty or protocol or by the adjudication of some authoritative body, such as the European Court of Human Rights. Such resolution does not, however, quell the normative debate about the nature and scope of particular human rights or of human rights in general. What we are witnessing is a broader cultural phenomenon in which the norms of human rights theory are in a state of constant revision and reassessment.

The same can be said of the *Compendium*. It can best be understood, not as some unchanging, constant, articulation of the rights and responsibilities of human beings in society but rather as a dynamic, ongoing assessment of this theme, in relation to which commentators can identify changes of emphasis over time. What is important to note about the *Compendium* however is that its absolutely core concept of the inherent dignity of every human being is constant and unchanging and enlightens the specific norms relating to social justice and the common good.

Human dignity

Human dignity[2] is not the core value of international human rights instruments.[3] The Preamble to the Charter of the United Nations in 1945 and the Preamble to the Universal Declaration on Human Rights in 1948 both refer to 'the dignity and worth of the human person'. Both the International Covenant on Civil and Political Rights and the International Covenant on Economic, Social and Cultural Rights recognise 'the inherent dignity and ... the equal and inalienable rights of all members of the human family' as the foundation of freedom, justice and peace in the world. Dignity is a value underlying the Irish Constitution. Indeed the Irish Constitution is the first, so far as I am aware, in which dignity is given such a role.

The concept of human dignity is of an ancient pedigree.[4] Its philosophical origins may be found in Greek philosophy and in Judeo-Christian insight into the unique value and equal worth of every human being.[5]

The *Compendium* states:

> A just society can become a reality only when it is based on the respect of the transcendent dignity of the human person. The person represents the ultimate end of society, by which it is ordered to the person: 'Hence, the social order and its development must invariably work to the benefit of the human person, since the order of

> things is to be subordinate to the order of persons, and not the other way around. Respect for human dignity can in no way be separated from obedience to this principle. It is necessary to 'consider every neighbour without exception as another self, taking into account first of all his life and the means necessary for living it with dignity.' Every political, economic, social, scientific and cultural programme must be inspired by the awareness of the primacy of each human being over society. (132)

Compendium values and human rights theory: four questions

It may be useful to contrast the approach of the *Compendium* to the relationship between rights, responsibilities and the common good with that adopted in contemporary human rights theory. What emerges is of some interest. The integration of these three concepts in the *Compendium*, inspired by the predominant notion of human dignity, is increasingly finding a mirror in contemporary human rights theory. The big issues relating to human rights over the past century have included the following four questions:

- Should a distinction be made between civil and political rights, on the one hand, and economic and social rights, on the other?
- Are human rights enforceable only against the state or can they also be enforced against non-state actors, even private citizens in their relationships with each other?
- Are there human responsibilities as well as rights?
- Should human rights be protected by states or by some wider, possibly global, authority?

Civil and political rights versus economic and social rights?

As to the first of these questions, as you know, the enmities of the Cold War led to the breaking up of human rights into two artificial categories, each with its own covenant. Thus we have the International Covenant on Civil and Political Rights and the International Covenant on Economic, Social and Cultural Rights. A sustained assault was made by some on the justiciability of economic, social and cultural rights, backed by arguments based on the separation of the powers doctrine and appeals to democratic values. This debate has found its way into Irish judicial circles.[6]

The Vienna Declaration and Programme of Action, in 1993, sought to remedy this artificial distinction, so far as possible. Paragraph 5 of the Declaration states:

> All human rights are universal, indivisible and interdependent and interrelated. The international community must treat human rights globally in a fair and equal manner, on the same footing, and with the same emphasis. While the significance of national and regional particularities and various historical, cultural and religious backgrounds must be borne in mind, it is the duty of states, regardless of their political, economic and cultural systems, to promote and protect all human rights and fundamental freedoms.

In Catholic social thought, there is no artificial distinction between civil and political rights and economic and social rights. Pope John Paul II in his message for the celebration of the World Day of Peace on 1 January 1999 made the following observations:

> All human beings, without exception, are equal in dignity. For the same reason, these rights apply to every stage of life and to every political, social, economic and cultural situation. Together they form a single whole, directed unambiguously towards the promotion of every aspect of the good of both the person and society.
>
> Human rights are traditionally grouped into two broad categories, including on the one hand civil and political rights and on the other economic, social and cultural rights. Both categories, although to different

> degrees, are guaranteed by international agreements. All human rights are in fact closely connected, being the expression of different dimensions of a single subject, the human person. The integral promotion of every category of human rights is the true guarantee of full respect for each individual right.
>
> Defence of the universality and indivisibility of human rights is essential for the construction of a peaceful society and for the overall development of individuals, peoples and nations. To affirm the universality and indivisibility of rights is not to exclude legitimate cultural and political differences in the exercise of individual rights, provided that in every case the levels set for the whole of humanity by the Universal Declaration are respected.

It is clear that Catholic social thought has no place for untrammelled 'democratic majoritarianism' without regard for social justice and the common good.

Rights against whom?

Let us now consider the second question: whether human rights are enforceable only against the state or may also be enforced against non-state actors. This is a matter of heated debate.[7] In Catholic social thought, there is no need to limit the obligation to respect human rights to states. Of course, those in society who are involved in the process of government, at all political levels, may have more wide-ranging authority and responsibilities than others, but only for the purpose of attaining the common good;[8] and everyone is required to make his or her own specific contribution to the general welfare. The trend in human rights theory is in the direction of expanding the range of those subject to the obligation to comply with human rights instruments. The state-based model of analysis is beginning to look somewhat jaded.

Human responsibilities

Let us turn to the third question. The great international human rights instruments of the United Nations speak largely the language of rights rather than duties. Article 29(1) of the Universal Declaration of Human Rights 1948 is exceptional in providing that '[e]veryone has duties to the community in which alone the free and full development of his personality is possible'. The African Charter on Human and Peoples' Rights[9] and the African Charter on the Rights and Welfare of the Child contain provisions spelling out duties and responsibilities as well as rights.

Catholic social theory involves a reciprocal relationship between rights and duties:

> Every basic human right draws its authoritative force from the natural law, which confers it and attaches to it its respective duty. Hence, to claim one's rights and ignore one's duties, or only half fulfil them, is like building a house with one hand and tearing it down with the other.[10]

The acknowledgement of our responsibility to society has become more easily recognised in certain aspects of our lives over the past couple of decades. We are now conscious of our environmental responsibilities to future generations; we have concerns about global warming; the smoking ban was a striking example of how the social dimension of our lives was considered sufficiently important to impose restrictions on our choices.

A global remit?

The fourth issue involves the question as to whether some supra-national, global body should be charged with task of protecting human rights. For decades, during the Cold War, there was little or no prospect that it could actually achieve this goal. Today, there are some indications of a strengthening of the notion of a global law. The International Criminal Court is a striking example of this trend.

Catholic social theory looks in the same direction, emphasising the need for the world community to act in harmony if the global common good is to be achieved:

> Today the universal common good presents us with problems which are world-wide in their dimensions; problems, therefore, which cannot be solved except by a public authority with power, organisation and means co-extensive with these problems, and with a world-wide sphere of activity. Consequently the moral order itself demands the establishment of some such general form of public authority ...
>
> The common good of individual states is something that cannot be determined without reference to the human person, and the same is true of the common good of all states taken together. Hence the public authority of the world community must likewise have as its special aim the recognition, respect, safeguarding and promotion of the rights of the human person.[11]

The migration of workers and their families between states requires us to adopt global principles of social justice. The International Convention on the Protection of the Rights of Immigrant Workers came into force on 1 July 2003, yet Ireland shows no immediate prospect of adopting it. The Convention seeks to protect the human rights of migrant workers and their families. No good argument in social justice has been, or could be, put forward against our adopting the Convention. This is an instance where human dignity must not be put in second place to economic profit.

Synthesis

What emerges from this brief consideration of these four issues is that human rights theory is moving from a model of civil and political rights held by citizens against states to a far more complex model of society, at every stage from individuals, private associations, local and national authorities to global institutions being in a recognised relationship of mutual rights and responsibilities, based on recognition of the primary value of human dignity. This is precisely the model that emerges from the *Compendium*. For those interested in the future development of human rights, it represents a most useful philosophical framework for analysis and debate.

The common good

Let us turn to consider the common good. It is a term that had widespread currency several decades ago in Ireland and it features strongly in the Constitution of 1937. Over the years, it would be fair to say that it lost a degree of currency. It came to be regarded as a conservative brake on the development of autonomy-based rights. With the removal of criminal prohibitions from a range of areas of autonomy-related action we can perhaps look again, and in a clearer way, at the notion of the common good. The first, and most obvious, point to note about it is that it has a huge impact in the area of social justice. It is rooted in 'the dignity, unity and equality of all people'.[12]

The following passage from *Gaudium et spes* is worth close consideration:

> Every day human interdependence grows more tightly drawn and spreads by degrees over the whole world. As a result the common good, that is, the sum of those conditions of social life which allow social groups and their individual members relatively thorough and ready access to their own fulfilment, today takes on an increasingly universal complexion and consequently involves rights and duties with respect to the whole human race. Every social group must take account of the needs and legitimate aspirations of other groups, and even of the general welfare of the entire human family.
>
> At the same time, however, there is a growing awareness of the exalted dignity proper to the human

> person, since he stands above all things, and his rights and duties are universal and inviolable. Therefore, there must be made available to all men everything necessary for leading a life truly human, such as food, clothing and shelter; the right to choose a state of life freely and to found a family, the right to education, to employment, to a good reputation, to respect, to appropriate information, to activity in accord with the upright norm of one's own conscience, to protection of privacy and rightful freedom, even in matters religious.
>
> Hence, the social order and its development must invariably work to the benefit of the human person if the disposition of affairs is to be subordinate to the personal realm and not contrariwise ...
>
> This social order requires constant improvement. It must be founded on truth, built on justice and animated by love; in freedom it should grow every day toward a more humane balance. An improvement in attitudes and abundant changes in society will have to take place if these objectives are to be gained. (26)

It is hard to read this passage and fail to appreciate how close it is to the language of the International Covenant on Economic, Social and Cultural Rights. That Covenant acknowledges that recognition of the inherent dignity and of the equal and inalienable rights of all the members of the human family is the foundation of freedom, justice and peace in the world and it recognises that these rights derive from the inherent dignity of the human person. The notion in *Gaudium et spes* that the social order 'requires constant improvement' and that 'in freedom it should grow every day toward a more human balance' echoes the theme of progressivity underlying the Covenant. Identifying rights to food, clothing, shelter, education and employment as integral to a life that is truly human finds parallels in the rights recognised in the Covenant.

Engaging the wider society

In my view, it would be helpful for the advancement of human rights protection if those who favour the values articulated in the *Compendium* could make it plain that these values are perfectly consistent with the language of international human rights instruments, especially the International Convention on Economic and Social Rights. I see two principal benefits. First, the advocacy for social justice would be more effective since it would soften prejudices that the advocate was speaking from some exclusively religious perspective. In fact the central values of contemporary human rights theory on social justice are to be found in the *Compendium*. Second, at the local level of Irish constitutional theory it might have the effect of opening the minds of some members of the judiciary to the argument that an active judicial role in response to the call of social justice, far from subverting democratic norms, would actually enrich our society and deepen the strength of our democracy.

Notes

1 See van der Vyver, 'The Concept of Human Rights: Its History, Contents and Meaning', [I979] *Acta Juridica* 10.

2 See D. Kretzmer and E. Klein (eds) 'The Concept of Human Dignity in Human Rights Discourse' (2002); Feldman, 'Human Dignity as a Legal Value' [1999] Public L 682 [2000] Public L 61.

3 See Dicke, 'The Founding Function of Human Dignity in the Universal Declaration of Human Rights', in D. Kretzmer and E. Klein (eds) op. cit., p. 111.

4 See Canick, 'Dignity of Man' and 'Persona' in 'Stoic Anthropology: Some Remarks on Cicero', *De Officiis* I, pp. 105–7, in D. Kretzmer and E. Klein (eds) op. cit., p. 19.

5 Cf. Starck, 'The Religious and Philosophical Background of Human Dignity and Its Place in Modern Constitutions' in D. Kretzmer and E. Klein (eds) op. cit., p. 179, at pp. 180–1 (footnote references omitted):

The recent affirmation of human dignity in constitutions

and international declarations is a product of a relatively secular age. Yet the development of the underlying idea – the concept of what a human being is – closely parallels the development of Christian thought. Both the Old and New Testaments state that the basis of human dignity is the fact that humans were created in the image of God (Gen 1:27; Eph 4:24). It follows that every human being has inalienable value in his or her own right, which is why no human being may be treated as a mere object or as a means to an end.

A second strand of the concept of human dignity finds its origins in classical antiquity. Philosophers in this period recognised characteristics of human beings that distinguish them from animals, namely their capacity for rational thought and free will, and from this starting point began to recognise human dignity in citizens. Later, their theory was extended in a more cosmopolitan context to all human beings.

A strong social component characterises the classical and Christian concepts of freedom which the notion of human dignity underpins: human beings were always seen as interdependent, social creatures. This is evident from the concepts of the polis, of the community of believers, of general fraternity and of solidarity. Human freedom was anchored in divine law, in natural law and in moral law.

Christian life and belief, in which human beings depend (religio) on God, on Jesus Christ as intercessor and saviour and on the Christian community, led by the Holy Spirit, transcend the physical world. In this context, it is usual to speak of metaphysics. Thus, human beings have a metaphysical anchor, which provides the basis for their freedom, and for their equality and fraternity: all human beings are, in equal measure, the image of God. Human dignity does not mean unlimited self-determination, but self-determination which is exercised on the basis that everyone – not simply the person claiming the right to self-determination – is of value in his or her own right.

6 See Sinnot v Minister for Education [2001] 2 IR 545, TD v Minister for Education [2001] IESC 101, critically analysed by

Gerard Whyte, *Social Inclusion and the Legal System: Public Interest Law in Ireland*, PA, 2002.

7 See Andrew Clapham, 'Human Rights Obligations of Non-State Actors', 2006, Wade, 'Horizons of Horizontality', 116 LQ Rev. 217, 2000. It is noteworthy that, in Irish constitutional theory, constitutional rights may be enforced not only against the state, but also against private individuals: Meskell v Coras Iompair Eireann [1973] IR 121. See further Binchy, 'Constitutional Remedies and the Law of Torts' in J. O'Reilly (ed.) *Human Rights and Constitutional Law: Essays in Honour of Brian Walsh*, 1992, p. 201.

8 *Pacem in terris*, 53.

9 Article 27 of the African Charter on Human and Peoples' Rights provides as follows:

Every individual shall have duties towards his family and society, the state and other legally recognised communities and the international community. 2. The rights and freedoms of each individual shall be exercised with due regard to the rights of others, collective security, morality and common interest.

Article 28 provides:

Every individual shall have the duty to respect and consider his fellow beings without discrimination, and to maintain relations aimed at promoting, safeguarding and reinforcing mutual respect and tolerance.

Finally, Article 29 provides:

The individual shall also have the duty: 1. To preserve the harmonious development of the family and to work for the cohesion and respect of the family; to respect his parents at all times, to maintain them in case of need; 2. To serve his national community by placing his physical and intellectual abilities at its service; 3. Not to compromise the security of the state whose national or resident he is; 4. To preserve and strengthen social and national solidarity, particularly when the latter is threatened; 5. To preserve and strengthen the national independence and the territorial integrity of his country and to contribute to its defence in accordance with the law; 6. To work to the best of his abilities and competence, and to pay taxes imposed by law in the interest of the society; 7. To preserve and strengthen positive African cultural values in his relations with other members of the society, in the spirit of tolerance, dialogue and consultation and, in general, to contribute to the promotion of the moral well-being of society; 8. To contribute to the best of his abilities, at all times and at all levels, to the promotion and achievement of African unity.

10 *Pacem in terris*, 30.
11 *Pacem in terris*, 139.
12 *Compendium*, 164.

11

DISABILITY AND DIFFERENCE:
The *Compendium* on the Inherent Dignity of the Human Person

Deirdre Carroll

Issues of disability have moved from the sidelines to ones of genuine interest and concern and are now today a legitimate topic for public debate in this country. This reflects the wider international movement for human and social rights for people with disabilities – a movement which has fought over the past five decades to counter the deep layers of prejudice and cultural influences which normalised the isolation and segregation of people with disabilities and which allowed the handing over of their care to people, some of whom did value their inherent humanity. Gerard Quinn, Professor of Law and Dean of the Faculty of Law at NUI Galway, who has published extensively on disability law, has pointed out that the application of the human rights approach in the field of disability is relatively new. He states that the human rights revolution in the context of disability has to do with making the human being visible and making the benefits of human rights and democracy available to all.[1]

The *Compendium* devotes a small but important section in Chapter 3 (148) to people with disabilities under the heading 'The Equal Dignity of All People'. It makes two key statements. The first says: 'Persons with disabilities are fully human subjects with rights and duties.' The second says: 'The rights of persons with disabilities need to be promoted with effective and appropriate measures.' The first statements mirrors closely the most famous of the international human rights instruments: the UN Universal Declaration of Human Rights (1948) which proclaims in its opening article that all human beings are born free and equal in dignity and rights. The second statement raises the more modern question of how we deal with difference in our world. In the last two decades there have been a number of international conventions, convenants and treaties drawn up to protect people, including people with disabilities, from abuse and discrimination. Many of these international instruments are legally binding on the states who ratified them and they are obliged to observe them. For example: the International Covenant on Economic, Social and Cultural Rights (1966), International Covenant on Civil and Political Rights (1966), the Convention against Torture and other Cruel, Inhuman or Degrading Treatment or Punishment (1984), the Convention on the Rights of the Child (1989); all of which have been ratified by the Irish government. In addition, many countries have introduced into their national law anti-discrimination legislation to protect the rights of marginalised groups. In Ireland the broad equality legislation of the late 1990s impacted on people with disabilities in their right not to be discriminated on the grounds of their disability in their access to employment and goods and services.

The *Compendium* with its emphasis on the rights of people with disabilities could be said to be part of this disability rights revolution. It does not see rights in a minimalist way. It speaks about how people with disabilities 'are to be helped to participate in every dimension of family and social life at every level accessible to them and according to their possibilities' (148). Human rights should not just be about protection against power but about restoring power to the person. To quote Professor Quinn, again when describing the importance of using rights to restore power to people:

> Economic, social and cultural rights have an enabling function: they provide a bridge whereby persons with disabilities can take their place as valued and often highly productive citizens.

The core principles at the heart of the rights-based perspective is that the real problem in relation to disabled people lies not with the person but in the way society treats the difference of disability. This is not to deny that differences exist but while all people are different they are, as the *Compendium* states, equal in the eyes of God and, as our constitution acknowledges, equal in the eyes of the law. This poses many challenges for us, and creating a society that recognises and values differences is not easy. The medical model of disability is still a dominant force in our society. This model defines people in terms of their physical deficiencies against a bench mark of some ideal type of norm of the able bodied. It has led to the creation of services dominated by the 'expert' or 'professional' whose job is to provide care and cure or the 'culture of care', as long-time disability campaigner Donal Toolan calls it.[2] Disabled people and their families were expected to participate in this process and, if they did not do so wholeheartedly enough or questioned what was being put in place for them, were either dismissed as not having come to terms with the reality of their condition or, as has happened and continues to happen, were told if they did not like what was on offer they could look elsewhere – a realistic option in a society where choices are few and rights non-existent.

Historically, services in Ireland have been provided under the medical model. Religious and charitable organisations dedicated to a single type of disability, 'the mentally handicapped', 'the deaf', 'the blind', provided care and services in the absence of any state provision. Their pioneering role in this area must be recognised and applauded. However, at the same time the traditional charitable model can be rightly viewed as a reactionary force in the development of a modern policy in relation to disability.[3] For example, the preoccupation of charities with private fundraising due to lack of inadequate state support and their perceived role as interpreters of what disabled people need.

The first major landmark in the breaking with this model in Ireland was the publication of the report of the Commission on the Status of People with Disabilities in 1996.[4] Chaired by Justice Flood, the Commission set out a radical programme for change on how services for people with disability are delivered, including a call for disability legislation which would establish rights for people with disabilities. This was indeed a major shift in philosophy when it is recalled that a little over ten years previously a Green Paper on services for people with disability, discussing the need for legislation, stated:

> The most important thing which any disadvantaged minority needs is good will and understanding ... the Government is convinced that the promotion of the rights of the disabled people can best be achieved by general agreement rather than by measures of compulsion.[5]

Today we have a Disability Act which was passed last year amidst much controversy after the government was forced to withdraw a previous bill in 2002. This was owing to the strength and sheer anger of the disability community at its contents and its attempt to prevent people having redress to the courts. This is an act which is considered by my members and many disabled people to fall far short of the vision imagined by the Commission. The Irish Human Rights Commission in their observations on the bill listed seventeen areas in which it could be improved upon. The Disability Legislation Consultation Group (established by government to consult on the new legislation) in May 2005 pointed to five core issues which they said must be addressed before the bill proved acceptable to people with disabilities and their families. In November 2005 the Ombudsman Ms Emily O'Reilly expressed concern that the wording of the act may not be robust enough to ensure that public bodies take sufficient steps to improve access for disabled people to buildings and services. The consensus is that the act is not an enabling piece of legislation which will assist people to be in control of their own lives. It represents the least the state can do for its disabled citizens, citing throughout phrases like 'where practicable' and having regard to 'resources and obligations'. The act is an opportunity lost. Lost because there was a deep-seated fear in certain quarters that to offer even the possibility of right to life-enhancing services over a specified time was to offer an open cheque book to already well-paid lawyers. In addition, the somewhat disturbing argument was put forward that enshrining rights in law for disabled people would deny the needs of others, such as the effective treatment of cancer patients or the care of the elderly.

Although there is now a much welcomed public commitment on the part of all politicians to improve the quality of life and opportunities for people with disabilities, including strong personal support from An Taoiseach Bertie Ahern, there is no doubt that the issue of rights-based legislation is not on the political agenda. However, we cannot continue to invest public monies in a system that lacks transparency, public accountability and which fails to prohibit practices which violate the human rights of many people with disabilities.

The recent scandals about the illegal charging of elderly people for long-stay care, which I may also add was happening to people with disabilities, and the appalling scandal of Leas Cross Nursing Home are examples of what happens when people are left to the vagaries of a system that had no legislative backbone. The practice of moving vulnerable disabled people to private nursing homes is still alive and well. These scandals have led to a call for an independent Social Services Inspectorate for elderly people. What most people do not know is that children and adults with disabilities in residential care have no protection from any type of inspectorate. Research shows that they are amongst the most vulnerable groups in our society and experience higher levels of abuse than others, such as children and the elderly. The delay in introducing standards for and inspections of disability services is one of many indicators to measure progress in developing a more inclusive society. Others include the well-documented high unemployment rates of disabled people and the number living below the poverty line.

Another issue of great concern to Inclusion Ireland [National Association for People with an Intellectual Disability] is the lack of any law in relation to guardianship or assisted decision making for vulnerable adults. The Law Reform Commission has also drawn attention to this problem in its recent publications on capacity and vulnerable adults. Inclusion Ireland's book *Who Decides and How*[6] explains these concerns in greater detail. If we and the government are serious about promoting change in this sector, significant changes must be made as to how services are provided and financed. This will require extra resources, but surely there has never been a better time in our history to do so. Above all, these changes must be underpinned by legislation which is clear and unambiguous and which has at its centre the rights of people with disabilities.

People with disabilities, their families and representatives groups have fought long and hard to get this issue on the political agenda. The reaction of the general public in the last few years has been heartening. It is such positive public support that will ultimately ensure the political will to give rights meaning for disabled people, not only in this country but throughout the world, as they fight for a new UN Convention on the Rights of Disabled People.

Note: The UN Convention on the Rights of Disabled People was passed in August 2006.

Notes

1 Quinn, G. with Bruce, A., 'Towards free and inclusive societies for people with disabilities' in Quin, S. and Redmond, B. (eds) *Disability and Social Policy in Ireland*, University College Dublin Press, 2003, p. 182.

2 'An emerging rights perspective for disabled people in Ireland: an activists view' in Quin, S. and Redmond B. (eds) ibid., p. 183.

3 Quin, S. and Redmond, B., ' Disability Policy in Ireland', ibid., pp. 1–9.

4 'Commission on the Status of People with Disabilities, A Strategy for Equality', The Stationery Office, Dublin, 1996.

5 Department of Health and Social Welfare, 'Towards a Full Life: A Green Paper on Services for Disabled People', The Stationery Office, Dublin, 1984, p. 112.

6 Dublin, 2003.

12

THE PRIVATISATION OF PUBLIC MORALITY: The *Compendium* on Religious Belief and Public Life

Nuala O'Loan

When asked to discuss the topic 'The Privatisation of Public Morality' I have to confess that I struggled a little as I sought the meaning of what I was being asked to talk about. As Police Ombudsman for Northern Ireland I will therefore discuss my experience of being a Catholic holding high office, the function of which is to call to account that which is probably the most powerful institution of the state – the police. My job is to investigate, independently and impartially, allegations of police criminality and police misconduct, whether those allegations come to me from citizens or from those responsible for policing and its governance: the Secretary of State, the Northern Ireland Policing Board, whose function is to ensure the delivery of effective, efficient policing, or the Chief Officer of policing – the Chief Constable. I also receive for investigation cases referred by coroners conducting inquests into sudden deaths from the Criminal Cases Review Commission, which examines where the person convicted alleges wrongful conviction. On occasion in such cases the Criminal Cases Review Commission will become aware of the possibility that a police officer or officers may have acted criminally either in conducting the original investigation or in giving evidence to the court. In such cases they will refer the matter to me. These are often very sensitive cases – I think for example of the case of a young man convicted of a sectarian murder during the Troubles, who served most of a lengthy life sentence before the Criminal

Cases Review Commission referred his case back to the Court of Appeal, at which his conviction was quashed. In the course of their investigation the Criminal Cases Review Commission became aware of the possibility that police officers had perverted the course of justice by forcing him to sign his confession. That matter was referred to my office and we investigated and found compelling evidence of serious police wrongdoing.

We have investigated many other very serious cases and as a consequence of our work police officers have been convicted, or dismissed, or resigned following investigation by my office. At the moment we are in the final stages of an investigation into an allegation by the father of a young man murdered by loyalists that these men had been involved in other murders while acting as police informants. Effectively what has been alleged is that the police knew that these people were involved in murders and allowed them to continue to act in this way because they were a useful source of information about the activities of their paramilitary colleagues. It is an allegation of state collusion in a series of horrific murders. It is a very serious allegation, and such allegations and perceptions of state wrongdoing, whether justified or not, can have the effect eventually of undermining confidence in the very institution of policing within the state.

My appointment as Police Ombudsman caused some comment for a variety of reasons, one of which is very simply that I am a Catholic. The distrust in sections of our community in the North of individuals based on their religious affiliation is fundamental to the inability of our divided people to live together. The fight waged by republican terrorism, which sought to overturn the partition of Ireland to create a United Ireland by force is rightly condemned, notwithstanding that it emerged at a time of significant repressions and exclusion of Catholics from housing and employment and public representation in the North. Similarly there is recognition that the security forces colluded with loyalist paramilitaries on occasion in the fight against militant republicans. That recourse to arms did not arise in the context in which the Church accepts that there is justification for armed resistance (as articulated in paragraph 401 of the *Compendium*). Our problem was, as has been the case on so many occasions in history, that the legitimate attempts by the state to impose the rule of law were corrupted by thought processes, which on many occasions saw militant Republicanism as synonymous with Catholicism, and on others saw militant Loyalism as synonymous with Protestantism. This was rarely articulated but it is inherent in what happens. As a Catholic therefore what I encountered was a mindset which said, as one politician articulated it, that 'no Catholic could do this job' because this job involved the investigation for criminal offences of one of the primary organisations of the state, the police. There emerged, over the years in Northern Ireland, a corrupted way of thinking, which led the majority of the population to view the police as 'theirs'. To criticise the police became almost a form of treason. Hence the view that 'no Catholic could do this job'. To this day there remains an element, on occasions significant, of that distrust in my ability to provide a service to all the people which is founded on integrity, impartiality and independence. I had such a conversation most recently with a prominent Protestant member of the community who congratulated me upon the achievements of my office and who stated readily that it would have been much easier for me and for my staff had I not been a Catholic.

That distortion of understanding of what it means to be a Catholic is, I think, in part responsible for the Troubles. The *Compendium* has a significant contribution to make to the better understanding by both Catholics and all other religions of what the Catholic faith demands of its followers and of the consequences of the understanding of a world in which there is too a moral order which is transcendent, absolute, universal and equally binding of all. Paragraph 396 of the *Compendium* articulates the great danger which may result if a state fails to realise that 'it is from the moral order that authority derives its power to impose obligations and its moral legitimacy, not from some arbitrary will or from the thirst for power'. Paragraph 397 goes on to discuss the need for recognition by authority of essential human and moral values which 'flow from the very truth of the human being and express and safeguard the dignity of the person, values which no individual, no majority and no state can ever create, modify or destroy'. These values, it states:

> do not have their foundation in provisional and changeable 'majority' opinions but simply must be recognised, respected and promoted as elements of an objective moral law, the natural law written in the human heart and as the normative point of reference for the civil law itself.

The *Compendium* states with great clarity:

> If as a result of the tragic clouding of the collective conscience, scepticism were to succeed in casting doubt on the basic principles of moral law, the legal structure of the state itself would be shaken to its very foundations, being reduced to nothing more than a mechanism for the pragmatic regulation of different and opposing interests.

It probably seems simplistic to you when I say that from enhanced understanding of the social doctrine of the Church can emerge those structures which will enable us to live together in harmony for the common good, recognising the validity of a ruling authority which:

> must guarantee an ordered and upright community life without usurping the free activity of individuals and groups but disciplining and orientating this freedom, by respecting and defending the independence of the individual and social subjects, for the attainment of the common good. (394)

We have not previously had ready access to the articulation of the teaching of the Church, in terms of social doctrine. The present volume is not the simplest to read. Footnotes in Latin will not enhance the understanding of a population, large sections of which no longer study or have any understanding of Latin. Translation of the footnotes is a necessary development for the *Compendium*. It will be important also that a way is found of communicating its contents to the world, both Catholic and non-Catholic, so that there will be a greater opportunity for enhanced understanding of the faithfulness of Catholic social doctrine to the scriptures.

I want to reflect briefly on the extent to which the Church itself, in its human frailty, has fallen short of its compliance with the demands of a moral order which is 'transcendent, absolute, universal and equally binding on all'. I am thinking now of those structures of the Church which seek to give effect to Canon Law in two sectors of activity which impact on ordinary people and priests. The first involves some consideration of the processes by which the Church decides upon the validity of individual marriages. Paragraph 404 of the *Compendium* discusses the requirements for proper investigation of criminal activity in terms which would be recognisable to most human rights lawyers. The *Compendium* identified, quoting Pope John Paul II in an Address to the Association of Italian Judges in 2000, the need to ensure that 'trials are conducted swiftly, and matters dealt with'. How applicable are such principles to Church Marriage Tribunals in which, for applicants from Northern Ireland at least, delays are inordinate and go largely unchallenged? I know one young woman who has been waiting ten years for the annulment of a marriage which lasted less than six months and in respect of which there were very few witnesses to interview and few opportunities for evidence gathering. All the evidence available is perceived to be absolutely compelling in its witness to the fact that this was no marriage. As this young woman waits, her life passes her by. It is not because this is how God has ordained it should be; it is because the Church in Ireland has failed to create the structures and mechanisms which would result in justice. I know of other similar cases, equally compelling, in which individuals are in limbo, where they, who seek to follow most faithfully the ordinances of the Church and of the Lord whom they love and seek to serve, experience at the hands of that Church another 'real injustice' similar to that of which John Paul II spoke. In allowing this situation to develop and to continue unchallenged, it seems to me that the Church in Ireland has failed in its duty to some of its people, in the most precious part of their lives: their relationship to others, to the community of the people of God and to the God who made them.

There is one final area about which I wish to speak and it is even more sensitive. We have all seen the terrible litany of the pain of those abused by a small number of members of our Church. The response of the Church in Ireland was inadequate and in some cases criminal – we saw the collusion which resulted in the movement of a few priests, known to be paedophiles, from parish to parish. It was wrong, terribly wrong. More recently we have seen a completely different approach, and there is much to be commended in the new rules here for how to deal with these matters. But it is my view that inherent in those new rules is another injustice which will cause equal harm. For it seems to me that whilst articulating the fact that people are innocent until proved guilty, the Church does not reflect this understanding in the way in which she deals with those accused, especially those accused of offences which allegedly occurred twenty and thirty years ago, which inevitably are much harder to investigate. Priests who are accused usually have to leave their homes and go away into what is effectively a desert in which they cannot function in the life to which they have been called. In cases where there is real evidence and a need to protect children this is absolutely right. In cases where there is a vague allegation, particularly where that allegation changes rapidly on the first few occasions on which it is recounted, it is wrong to deprive men of their character and way of life. I have investigated such allegations against police officers. The police investigate similar allegations against civilians. If those allegations are proved to be false, or if they are unproven, the accused goes back into their professional life. Such accusations cause huge distress to the accused as well as the accuser, but at the end of the investigation, those falsely accused will be able to get on with their lives. In many cases in the Church here in Ireland, this does not happen. And men against whom the evidence is simply not to be found will nevertheless not be permitted to return to work, but will spend the rest of their days waiting. For what? I know of many such men living apart in monasteries and seminaries for whom life is on hold indefinitely because the Church does not have in place the structures to enable proper handling of the issue. This is wrong.

Where the Church responds disproportionately in situations such as those to which I have referred above, it is not true to the Gospel. It, too, is privatising that morality which should underpin all its activities and in so doing becoming less faithful. The Church should be alert to those situations in which it may become responsible for the perpetration of grave injustice. The *Compendium* is a rich resource for those for whom the call to holiness is lived as they work in the fields of justice and human rights both within the Church and outside it. As Cardinal Bemardin wrote: 'We will serve others when we walk with them in the dark valleys of oppressive structures.' After my initial struggle to discern what this *Compendium* means for me personally, I now know that there is much to ponder on within it. As Police Ombudsman I have always felt that my calling is 'to act justly, to love tenderly and to walk humbly'.

13

GLOBAL MOVEMENTS OF PEOPLE: The *Compendium* on the Rights of the Family

Joan Roddy

The Palestinian academic, Edward Said, poignantly described exile as 'compelling to think about but terrible to experience'.[1] Here is someone, himself an exile, who knew this experience in his flesh and bones. But we do not have to move as far away as the Middle East to find touching descriptions of exile. For example, the words of playwright and novelist, Eugene McCabe:

> It was Sunday when Paddy (twenty years old) phoned and asked: 'What's it like at home now ... the weather?' 'Raining', I said. 'Raining here too in Manhattan.' And we talked on. Near the end of the call he said: 'I've been looking down the street all morning thinking about Drumard, going round and round every field in my head, I can see them as clear as anything.' After that image of grieving it was hard to keep talking.[2]

The recent report of the Global Commission on International Migration[3] draws attention to the increase in the scale and scope of international migration and notes that 'there are now almost 200 million international migrants, a number equivalent to the population of Brazil, the fifth most populous country on earth'. This is more than double the figure recorded in 1980, just twenty-five years ago. Other recent figures indicate that, of those 200 million, some 10 million are refugees (down from 17 million in 2000) and 25 million are persons displaced within the borders of their own countries. The *Compendium* in several places draws attention to the situation of migrants and displaced persons. The introduction (17) notes that one of the great challenges facing humankind today is that of globalisation:

> Globalisation, which has flung markets wide open but not frontiers, has demolished boundaries for the free circulation of information and capital, but not to the same extent those for the free circulation of people.[4]

The *Compendium*, of course, also repeatedly refers to the role of the family, which is a key theme in Catholic social teaching. It states unequivocally that 'it is impossible to promote the dignity of the person without showing concern for the family' (185). So, in the context of the millions of people globally on the move today – be they migrant workers, refugees or others – none can be looked at apart from the family to which she or he belongs, whatever the configuration of that family. Human rights, the right to a dignified life, cannot then be assured by looking at a person simply as an individual, in isolation from her or his family. On the other hand, neither can human rights themselves be respected if taken individually or in isolation from one another. Let us again look to the *Compendium*: 'Human rights are to be defended not only individually but also as whole ... Universality and indivisibility are distinctive characteristics of human rights ...' (154) Bishop Donal Murray put this very succinctly, but goes further when he says:

> ... human rights are unconditional and inalienable. To respect them is to respond not just to one's equals but to God ... in some sense, the claims of another human being are the claims of God.[5]

Perhaps we can best look at all of this – the social doctrine of the Church and today's global realities – through the lives of some individual people. Pierre[6] came to Ireland seeking asylum in December 2000. In his home country in French-speaking West Africa he was an active member of an opposition party and he believes that to return there, under a military regime, will result in certain imprisonment and probable death. His first interview in the asylum process, over four year ago, was taking place just as a major happening of global significance became 'breaking news' here. From the time this news became known (during a pause in the interview), in Pierre's own words, 'the nature of the interview changed completely and, from my point of view, went downhill'. A year later, just some twenty minutes before his appeal hearing, Pierre, meeting a solicitor for the first time, was asked for details of his case. Pierre explains: 'I knew I would be unable to put my case through the interpreter in this brief time. It was such an important day for me and I felt really helpless.' His appeal was unsuccessful and he was later issued with a deportation order.

Today, five years and two months after his arrival in Ireland, Pierre awaits the outcome of the judicial review of the order for his deportation, a judgment which has already been postponed several times. His solicitor, rightly, keeps reminding him that there are no criteria by which to assess whether the Minister for Justice, Equality and Law Reform [then Michael Mc Dowell] will reconsider his decision to deport this man. To that extent, it inevitably feels to Pierre as if the decision will be arbitrary. In the meantime, Pierre continues to avail of any training courses open to him and has earned certificates to prove it, as well as references from various places where he has volunteered, including the charity shop in which he is currently involved. However, not being allowed as an asylum seeker to take up regular paid employment is a great drawback from many viewpoints – he recognises this, but has chosen to comply with official regulations in the hope that this will be to his advantage in the long-run. Likewise, he continues to report on a regular basis to the Garda National Immigration Bureau.

This man of almost forty-two years, a son, brother, husband

and father, has not seen any of his family for over five years and communication with them is, at best, erratic. For Pierre, the greatest challenge of each day is to continue to dare to believe that he has a future.

Just ten days ago [21 February 2006] the United Nations High Commissioner for Refugees[7] had this to say:

> The number of refugees worldwide ... is at its lowest level in almost a quarter century ... Yes, the decline in the number of refugees reflects peace agreements and positive developments in several countries ... But at the same time, I fear that it also reflects the barriers which have been erected by states seeking to deter and control irregular migration. These barriers are not necessarily aimed at refugees but they do not differentiate between them and other categories of people on the move. And the less they differentiate, the fewer genuine refugees will overcome them.
>
> The reasons people are on the move are complex ... A more consistent approach to refugee protection in the EU ... should not lead to a lowering of standards, to a convergence around the lowest common denominator ... Europe is – and must remain – a continent of asylum.

And the High Commissioner goes on to quote Lord Patten:

> Former Commissioner Chris Patten wrote recently of his hope for Europe to define itself as a symbol of tolerance. 'Tolerance', Lord Patten said, should be the 'element that defines our European Community'.

The High Commissioner also drew attention to the situation of people displaced within the borders of their own countries. Their numbers have increased – to an estimated 25 million, mostly women and children. However poorly it sometimes operates, there is for refugees a legal and institutional framework designed to protect them. But there is no similar architecture for the internally displaced who are invariably living in countries beset by poverty and political turbulence. Their situation is one of extreme vulnerability, which lacks any immediate hope of improvement. The Church's social teaching highlights the fact that the individual person or family cannot on their own secure all that is necessary to lead a full life: they need the support of political and social institutions to have access to material, cultural, moral and spiritual goods necessary for a truly human life (168). The *Compendium* states clearly 'there is still ... much hesitation in the international community about the obligation to respect and implement human rights...' (365).

Let us look through another window, this time with the help of the current issue of a respected information bulletin on Immigrants and Refugees.[8] In France, the Minister of the Interior has on several occasions affirmed his wish to put in place selective immigration, instead of having immigration 'imposed' on France. He wants to do away with some of the existing rights of immigrants. '(S)elected or chosen foreigners will be given preferential treatment ... it is proposed they be issued with a special residence permit called "capabilities and talents".' But the *Compendium* says:

> Society should never fail in its fundamental task of respecting and fostering the family. Society, and in particular state institutions ... [are] called to guarantee and foster the genuine identity of family life ... This requires political and legislative action to safeguard family values. (252)

In the Netherlands, the Minister for Immigration secured the support of a parliamentary majority for a new measure requiring would-be immigrants to pass an integration test before even being admitted to the country. The tests will be carried out at a Dutch Embassy or Consulate and would-be immigrants will be required to show a certain level of knowledge of Dutch language and Dutch culture. Their knowledge will be tested over the phone, using a personal computer with speech recognition software. When individual migrants must meet such stringent requirements, how can the 'priority of the family' – on which the *Compendium* insists – be assured:

> The recognition on the part of civil society and the state of the priority of the family over every other community ... means ... accepting the family dimension as the indispensable cultural and political perspective in the consideration of persons ... people must not be considered only as individuals but also in relation to the family nucleus to which they belong. (254)

In evaluating whether a person has the financial resources to support family members in Denmark without recourse to social welfare, the authorities there will now take into account the visa applicant's personal property in the country of origin. However, couples wishing to start their own business will be granted dispensation. These examples suggest a trend in European countries to place their own interests and requirements, both economic and social, before the interests and well-being of immigrants. Where in this process is the place for the values and principles highlighted in the *Compendium* when it refers to 'the family dimension as the indispensable cultural and political perspective' within which the individual is thought about (254)?

Against this backdrop of the Church's social doctrine, mention must be made of the recent scheme[9] of the Department of Justice, Equality and Law Reform which permitted foreign parents of Irish children to apply for residency in Ireland, but with the proviso (involving a Statutory Declaration) that being granted permission to remain in the state would not 'give rise to any legitimate expectation ... that any ... family members abroad will as a result be given permission to remain in the state'. Effectively this means that an Irish citizen child can be deprived of the company of sisters and brothers and even of one parent. Ireland's failure to recognise the priority of family relationships is evident on an even greater scale in relation to the now large numbers of migrant workers in this country.

> The family is presented in the Creator's plan as the 'primary place of "humanisation" for the person and society' and the 'cradle of life and love'. (209)

> The Church considers the family as the first natural society, with underived rights that are proper to it ... Relegating the family 'to a subordinate or secondary role, excluding it from its rightful position in society, would be to inflict grave harm on the authentic growth of society as a whole'. (211)

Sergio is from a non-EU country in Central Europe. He came here three years ago, without a work permit, and, like many of his compatriots, works in the construction industry. When he left home, his wife was expecting their first baby. He has never seen, much less held, his two-year-old son whom he knows only from photographs and from cries, laughter and first halting words heard over the phone. Sergio longs to see his family, but he cannot go there and they cannot come here. For him, to risk not getting back into Ireland is unthinkable, given the whole family's dependence on his remittances. Fear of his identity being discovered means that in the workplace he must speak always the language of his 'assumed' country of origin and, among other things, be ahead of the Irish media with news of that country's football teams! On his birthday, when his father phoned while he was on the work site, he could not reply since he could not risk other workers hearing him speak in his other tongue.

It is important to note here that, in reality, there is a variety of circumstances which can lead someone to become undocumented. Many people, unwittingly and through no fault of their own, find themselves in an irregular situation, with grave consequences for their families, be they with them or in their country of origin. The comment of Max Frisch[10] – 'We wanted workers, but it was human beings who came' – seems all too applicable to Ireland today. The reluctance of Ireland, as indeed of many other developed countries, to face up to the responsibility of recognising family rights of migrants workers is, of course, linked with underlying negative attitudes towards immigration. As the Report of the Global Commission on Migration points out:

> In some parts of the world, negative attitudes towards migrants persist, despite the fact that entire sections of the economy depend on foreign labour.[11]

Church teaching is clear in its appreciation of the potential value of migration for both receiving and sending countries.

> Immigration can be a resource for development rather than an obstacle to it. In the modern world, where there are still grave inequalities between rich countries and poor countries, and where advances in communications quickly reduce distances, the immigration of people looking for a better life is on the increase ... In most cases ... immigrants fill a labour need which would otherwise remain unfilled in sectors and territories where the local workforce is insufficient or unwilling to engage in the work in question. (297)
>
> All people are called to become more and more aware that the need of industrialised countries for manpower is being answered by human beings: men, women and whole families with children and elderly people.[12]

Here, we cannot but recall the appeal by the 2003 Vatican World Congress on Migrants and Refugees to the Holy See and to governments to ratify as soon as possible the UN Convention on the Protection of the Rights of Migrant Workers and All Members of their Families.[13]

> His irregular legal status cannot allow the migrant to lose his dignity, since he is endowed with inalienable rights, which can neither be violated or ignored.[14]

In a speech which will surely find a place in the next edition of the *Compendium* – it was too late for this one! – Pope Benedict XVI noted that: '(T)here are increasingly more immigrants from less-privileged areas, in search of better conditions of life ... placing a growing number of them in situations of illegality.'[15] The Pope goes on to ask that the institutions of the host country take care that they not be considered as merchandise or a simple work force, and that their fundamental rights and human dignity be respected.

> Regulating immigration according to criteria of equity and balance is one of the indispensable conditions for ensuring that immigrants are integrated into society with the guarantees required by recognition of their human rights. Immigrants are to be received as persons and helped, together with their families, to become a part of societal life. In this context, the right of reuniting families should be respected and promoted. (298)

Let us leave the final word – and sentiment – to Eugene McCabe:

> It was our cousin, Michael O'Grady (twenty years in Arizona) who inherited his widowed mother's cottage in a village in Co. Clare. Sometimes, he said, he'd dial the number from Phoenix, just to hear the phone ringing three thousand miles away, in that empty room in Kildysart.[16]

Notes

1 Edward W. Said, *Reflections on Exile and other Essays*, Harvard University Press, 2000, quoted in Paul Surlis, 'Exile', *The Furrow*, April 2000, p. 203.

2 Eugene McCabe in *Sources* (ed. by Marie Heaney) Townhouse, Dublin, 1999, p. 158.

3 'Migration in an Interconnected World: New Directions for Action', October 2005, p. 1

4 'The Love of Christ towards Migrants', 4, Instruction of the Pontifical Council for the Pastoral Care of Migrants and Itinerant People, 2004.

5 *The Theological Basis of Human Rights,* pp. 17; 12, 'Human Rights', note 7, Irish Commission for Justice and Peace, 1998.

6 All names of persons have been changed to safeguard their identity.

7 Statement by Mr António Guterres United Nations High Commissioner for Refugees, to the European Parliament, Brussels, 21 February 2006 (circulated by Irish Refugee Council, 28 February 2006).

8 Migration News Sheet, Migration Policy Group, Brussels, February 2006, pp. 5–7.

9 'Application for permission to remain on the basis of parentage of an Irish-born child born before 1 January 2005', Department of Justice, Equality and Law Reform, Form: IBC/05.

10 Quoted by Ms Martina Liebsch (Chair, Caritas Europe Migration Commission) at Caritas Europe Migration Forum, Escorial, Spain, June 2003.

11 'Migration in an Interconnected World: New Directions for Action', Report of the Global Commission on International Migration, October 2005, p. 1.

12 'The Love of Christ towards Migrants', 42.

13 'Starting Afresh from Christ: Towards a Renewed Pastoral Care for Migrants and Refugees', Fifth World Congress on the Pastoral Care of Migrants and Refugees, Rome, 17–22 November 2003.

14 Message of Pope John Paul II for World Migration Day 1996.

15 Vatican News Service, 21 February 2006, quoted in Catholic Information Service for Africa, (CISA), 22 Feb 2006.

16 Eugene Mc Cabe, op. cit., p. 158.

14

TILLING THE GARDEN:
The *Compendium* on Caring for the Environment

Sylvia Thompson

> The earth is the Lord's and all that is in it, the world and those who live in it; for God has founded it on the seas, and established it on the rivers.
>
> Who shall ascend the hill of the Lord? And who shall stand in his holy place? Those who have clean hands and pure hearts, who do not lift up their souls to what is false, and do not swear deceitfully. They will receive blessing from the Lord and vindication from the God of their salvation. (Ps 24:1-5)
>
> ... and God saw that it was good. (Gen 1:4)

Biblical aspects

In the opening words of Chapter 10, 'Safeguarding the Environment', we read: 'The living experience of the divine presence in history is the foundation of the faith of the people of God.' This historical beginning is associated with Abram (Abraham). This leads one to think about those who preceded Abram and then to the opening chapter of the Gospel of John (1:1-5):

> In the beginning was the Word, and the word was with God, and the word was God. He was in the beginning with God. All things came into being through him, and

> without him not one thing came into being. What has come into being with him was life, and the life was the light of all people. The light shines in the darkness, and the darkness did not overcome it.

The *Compendium* reflects this hope because this divine presence from the beginning permits us 'to look to the future with hope, sustained by the promise and the covenant that God continually renews' (451). Clearly this hope is dynamic and needs to be both creative and responsive. It is certainly not a 'sitting back and hoping things will be alright' kind of hope. This arises from a constitutive part of our human identity – our relationship with the world – which is the result of that still-deeper relationship, our relationship with God. So there is no letting us off the hook of our duty 'to till and keep the garden', as not even sin permits us to stray from this, even if weighed down with pain and suffering (452). This world is the place of our salvation, so our challenge is to facilitate its radical purification which will make it a renewed world.[1]

Guiding principles and road maps?

But guidance, guiding principles, role models and maps are needed. One wonders if the *Compendium* said enough or is it just the aperitif? I was reminded of an incident that happened many years ago on the campus of Syracuse University in New York State. Maintenance people had been asked to repair the front steps of the library but as they were starting their work they became aware of some noise coming from around the back, which they went to investigate. There they found a different work crew had started their job: the demolition of the library, which was no longer able to sustain the weight of the books! The Columban priest and eco-theologian Fr Sean McDonagh commented that perhaps a more appropriate title for the conference would be 'The Common Good in an Unsustainable World'. Let us hope we are not just working on those front library steps!

This section closes with the call to all Christians 'to serve Christ, to live according to his Spirit, guided by love, the principle of a new life, that brings the world and man back to their original destiny' (455).

The nature of our relationship with the earth

This chapter of the *Compendium* goes on to address the more difficult issue of the nature of our relationship with the earth. It says that man shares in 'the light of the divine mind' and that today 'especially with the help of science and technology, man has extended his mastery over nearly the whole of nature and continues to do so'. There is much comfort to be had in our calling '... to govern the world with justice and holiness, a mandate to relate himself and the totality of things to him who was to be acknowledged as the Lord and Creator of all' (456). It goes on to stress our call to greater responsibility as 'the greater man's power becomes, the farther his individual and community responsibility extends' (457) i.e. saying the '... Church is in no way opposed to progress [953]' but rejoices in '... technological and economic progress which people, using their intelligence, have managed to make'. '... science and technology are a wonderful product of a God-given human creativity' (457) [and] 'could be a priceless tool in solving many serious problems' [but] 'it is necessary to maintain an attitude of prudence, and attentively sift out the *nature, end and means* of the various forms of applied technology.' (458 [959]) (emphasis in original)

In 1986 Pope John Paul II noted that 'scientists must truly put their research and technical skill in the service of humanity' (456). Two years later with the publication of *Solicitudo rei socialis* he calls for greater caution, stating that even when thought is given to making some change in them, 'one must take into account the nature of each being and of its mutual connection in an ordered system' (459). The *Compendium* says: 'A central point of reference for every scientific and technological application is respect for men and women which must be accompanied by a necessary attitude of respect for other living creatures' (459). We need to be mindful of our place in the great scheme of things. It is always based on God's 'prior and original gift of the things that are' (460). And this is a phrase we all need to heed:

> He must not make arbitrary use of the earth, subjecting it without restraint to his will as though it did not have its own requisites, and a prior God-given purpose which man can indeed develop but must not betray.' Because when he acts in this way 'instead of carrying out his role as a co-operator with God in the work of creation, man sets himself up in place of God and thus ends up provoking a rebellion on the part of nature, which is more tyrannised than governed by him. (460)

A crisis of relationship

The *Compendium* says the underlying cause of this crisis in relationship is 'man's pretension of exercising unconditional dominion' resulting in a view of the world as resource rather than home. It says this is '... the result of a long historical and cultural process' (461). It tries to strike a balance in how it wants believers to understand nature: not in a reductionist way i.e. nature as a mere object to be manipulated and exploited, and on the other hand 'not to absolutise nature and place it above the dignity of the human person' (463). It calls for an ever-greater need to respect the transcendent dimension of the human person and creation, and believes that the breakdown in this has ruptured various relationships – the world to God and man to the world – and has resulted in impoverishing man's very identity (464). It refers to both Benedictine and Franciscan spirituality, which have fostered a sort of kinship with his creaturely environment, thus fostering in us 'an attitude of respect for every reality of the surrounding world' (Pope John Paul 1997) (464).

In closing this section the *Compendium* says that if the new scientific capabilities are combined with a strong ethical dimension, the environment can be promoted as a home 'for man and for all men'. However, in my opinion, it stops there.

A call to a mature responsibility

The *Compendium* reminds us that the call to care for the environment, which represents 'a challenge for all of humanity' (466), is a responsibility that needs to mature on the basis of the global dimension of the present ecological crisis, since it states that all beings are interdependent in the universal order established by the Creator. It further states that the nature of each being and its mutual connection in an ordered systems must be taken into account. This leads into what, in my opinion, is sadly a rather brief reference to the environmental value of biodiversity and the need for this to be handled with a sense of responsibility and to be adequately protected. It also writes of the threat to this by actions such as destruction of forests, which leads to desertification and negative consequences for water reserves and compromises the lives of many indigenous peoples and the well-being of future generations.

All individuals as well as institutions must, according to the *Compendium*, feel the commitment to protect the heritage of forests and, where necessary, promote adequate programmes of reforestation. I did not find this to be a particularly strong call. It recognises that this call extends not only to present needs but to future needs. It sees that laws are an essential ingredient in this but not enough and that these must be accompanied by a growing sense of responsibility as well as an effective change of mentality and lifestyle. The 'precautionary principle' makes a welcome appearance in n. 469, recognising that science is often not able to come to quick conclusions about the absence of risk. It also states here that the decision-making process needs to be transparent. I find it alarming that such prudence is lacking. (In our recent, brief submission to the Environmental Protection Agency (EPA) about the introduction of genetically modified seeds and such into Ireland we in the Kerry Diocesan Justice, Peace and Creation Committee called for exercise of this principle.)

In this chapter of the *Compendium*, biotechnology is seen as a source of hope and enthusiasm on one hand and of alarm and hostility on the other and it states that 'Christians are not indifferent to these problems, for they are aware of the values at stake' (472). It offers some guidelines about such intervention.

In n. 473 I found somewhat puzzling statements:

> The Christian vision of creation makes a positive judgement on the acceptability of human intervention in nature, which also includes other living beings and at the same time makes a strong appeal for responsibility.

> The human person does not create an illicit act when out of respect for the order, beauty and usefulness of individual living beings and their function in the ecosystem he intervenes by modifying some of their characteristics or properties.

It stresses the need to evaluate accurately the real benefits as well as the possible consequences in terms of risks and it does say that it is unacceptable to act lightly or irresponsibly. But I was now left confused as I tried to reconcile the calls from the Pope, referred to earlier, to take into account a) 'the nature of each being' and b) 'its mutual connection in an ordered system'. [On the day, a slide was shown of a sheep: a reference to Dolly.] Maybe the guidelines offered may help: the Compendium states that 'nature ... is a gift ... entrusted to the intelligence and moral responsibility of man and woman' (473) and the chapter calls on the ethical evaluation of the modern biotechnologies and above all the criteria of justice and solidarity including equitable commercial exchange and the fostering of a necessary scientific and technological autonomy especially with regard to developing countries.

Staying with biotechnologies, in the area of food supply and healthcare, which activity involves material that 'belongs to the patrimony of humanity and is also destined to future generations', here it says that it hopes that scientists will employ their energies and abilities in research 'characterised by enthusiasm and guided by a clear and honest conscience'. And in calling on entrepreneurs and public agency directors to guide developments towards promising ends, i.e. the fight against hunger and disease and to safeguard the ecosystem, it calls this ecosystem 'the common patrimony of all' (478). However, it says we must avoid falling into unjustified alarmism but that society needs information that is complete and objective (480).

Climate, environment and the sharing of goods

Earlier in n. 470 the climate is termed as 'a good that must be protected' and the environment is also described as one of 'those goods that cannot be adequately safeguarded or promoted by market forces'. There is a call, though not particularly strong, to encourage the seeking of innovative ways to reduce the environmental impact of production and consumption of goods. It sees that climate change must be opportunely and constantly monitored at the scientific, political and juridical, national and international levels. It calls for non-renewable energy resources to be put at the service of all humanity and for research into the identification of new energy sources to be based on equity and intergenerational solidarity and that this should be illuminated and guided by continual reference to the universal common good. Here there is a particular mention of the relationship of indigenous peoples to their lands which is tied to the very meaning of their existence and resources not only to be protected, though many have been already lost or destroyed. These people are seen to offer an example of a life lived in harmony with the environment (471).

This section reminds us strongly that the goods of the earth were created by God to be used wisely by all and that they must be shared equitably, in accordance with justice and charity (481). It reminds us that the present environmental crisis especially affects those who are poorest. It speaks of those forced to live in the slum lands or polluted suburbs, countries penalised by unfair trade regulations, often making further environmental degradation even more likely. It touches too on the difficult question of uneven distribution of population and of available resources creating obstacles to development and a sustainable use of the environment, saying that all development worthy of the name must be 'integral', i.e. 'directed to the true good of every person and of the whole person'.

It acknowledges the right to safe drinking water 'as a universal and inalienable right' and so states that even if entrusted to the private sector it should still be considered as a public good. Finally, there is a call for new lifestyles in which the quest for 'truth, beauty, goodness and communion with others' for the sake of the common good are the factors that determine consumer choices, savings and investments. It calls for agricultural and industrial production that respect the order of creation and satisfy the basic human needs of all. It sees this crisis as a time for motivation for 'an authentic solidarity of worldwide dimensions'.

To end, I quote some words from the final paragraph:

> If ... nature is rediscovered in its creaturely dimension, channels of communication with it can be established, its rich and symbolic meaning can be understood, allowing us to enter into its realm of mystery. This realm opens the path of man to God, Creator of heaven and earth. The world presents itself before man's eyes as evidence of God, the place where God's creative, providential and redemptive power unfolds.

***Note*:** The author would have welcomed a more inclusive use of language in the text of the *Compendium*, a point that was also raised from the floor during the conference.

Note

1 From Leonardo and Clovodis Boff's 'Introducing Liberation Theology', taken from Donal Neary SJ, *Pilgrim in Lent*, Columba Press, 2000, p. 25.